THE ULTIMATE
Birthday Party Book

50 Complete and Creative Themes to
Make Your Kid's Special Day Funtastic!

Susan Baltrus

RIVER
OAK
PUBLISHING

The Ultimate Birthday Party Book:
50 Complete and Creative Themes to Make Your Kid's Special Day Funtastic!
ISBN 1-58919-900-6
46-615-00000
Copyright © 2002 by Susan Baltrus

Published by RiverOak Publishing
P.O. Box 700143
Tulsa, Oklahoma 74170-0143

Dedication

This book is dedicated to my courageous brother,

Steve Goretti,

and to my loving children,

Lauren, Sam, and Jillian.

Acknowledgements

I am grateful to the dozens of creative parents who shared their innovative ideas and diverse party philosophies with me. Your contributions have made this book what it is—a collection of ideas that reflects a broad range of party-giving styles. Thank you! A special thanks is due to the friends listed below.

Cindy Baratta
Pat Blanch
Jay Brady
Lydia Brady
Sheila Buckley
Leonora Cilento
Maureen Coneys
Nadine Evans
Paula Fahey
Joe Flatley
Cheryl Pearlman Fujii
Mary Giurleo
Christine Goretti
Steve Goretti
Kathy Griffin
Pat Johanson
Trish Homer
Carleen LaVita
Donna Magliozzi
Kate Merrigan
Mary McCann
Cheryl Morin
Carol O'Neill
Susan Pearlman
Ron Romano
Stephanie Rooney
Louise Tharrett
I am grateful to my editor, Shawna McMurry, for her continual support and vision.

Table of Contents

Introduction

Is there anything more exciting or more significant to young children than the celebration of a birthday? Birthdays are truly momentous occasions in the eyes of our children; and because we love our children, we strive to make their birthday celebrations memorable and special.

Many parents search for unique ways to mark the auspicious occasion. Some parents hire polished entertainers, some outsource the celebration to a party place, and some rent expensive equipment like moonwalks. Though outside sources can sometimes be helpful, a successful birthday party doesn't require any of these things. All you need are some creative ideas and a personalized approach that will reflect your child's interests. Children and their friends want a party that is unique and fun. They are less likely to remember the moonwalk or the slush machine than they are to remember the great time they had together and the personal attention you put into the special day.

Families today lead hectic and fast-paced lives, and many parents have precious little time or energy for party planning. After all, it's difficult to come up with all the ideas that make a birthday party complete. Outsourcing your child's party may be a viable option for some parents, but many parents want to simplify and personalize their child's celebrations, not commercialize them.

This book is a collection of creative birthday party ideas for parents who want to throw memorable parties that kids will love, without going overboard and without spending a fortune. It will give parents all the information they need to throw contemporary, well-thought-out, successful parties. It is jam-packed with ideas that are simple and inexpensive, yet fun and unique. Best of all, they don't require a week of set-up time!

The core of this book presents fifty different party themes, along with the steps to make each one come alive, from invitations and activities to cakes and favors. The book opens with an easy-to-follow question-and-answer section on party-throwing basics, and closes with tips for parties outside the home.

The ideas in this book came from parents just like you. I interviewed more than a hundred parents, asking them to tell me about the best children's birthday parties they had hosted or their kids had been invited to. What worked? What didn't? What left a lasting impression? I further probed the parents on their perceptions, viewpoints, and attitudes toward children's birthday parties.

Parents have an incredibly broad array of party-giving styles, ranging from casual, spontaneous get-togethers to carefully orchestrated productions. They each have their own rules of thumb. Some advise, "Invite as many guests as the age of your child," or "Don't open gifts at the party." Others have said, "The party shouldn't exceed one-and-a-half hours in length," and "Crafts are the best activities to begin a party." While their philosophies may work for them, they won't necessarily work for everyone. That's why I've put this book together. You can hear from all the parents—collectively, these parents have thrown several hundred birthday parties—and you can decide what's right for you and for your child.

The diversity of party-giving styles was just the beginning. These generous parents offered dozens of great ideas for making birthday parties fun. They also helped me realize that while a great cake, festive decorations, and a fancy invitation can add to the fun of a party, what's most important is what the children do once they're there. The games and activities make or break the party; so there's more to giving a successful birthday party than setting your table with matching plates and napkins and hanging streamers and balloons.

This book has been designed to be a user-friendly guidebook. Organized by theme, all the information you need for each party is all in one place. Each party has ideas for invitations, activities, decorations, cake, and party favors. This makes it easy for you to quickly scan the collection of parties to find one that reflects your child's interests, and then to check out all the suggestions for incorporating the theme. These ideas are just a starting point, though. They're likely to inspire you to dream up some creative ideas of your own.

You'll also find that this book will be a valuable reference guide for years to come. There are parties for kids from ages 2 to 12. There are party ideas for celebrations held inside the home and outside the home. There is a wide range of party themes that will appeal to the diverse interests of today's children—from a Victorian tea party to bugs to the color purple. This book is bound to have something for every child.

Perhaps most importantly, this book takes a realistic view of today's parents and how much time and money they are able to spend on planning and throwing birthday celebrations. The parties in this book are easy to throw, as well as a blast to attend. Their simplicity will amaze you! You'll read about secrets for creating simple fun that makes a party memorable.

By using the ideas in this book to create a personalized celebration for your child's birthday, not only will you make him or her feel honored and special, you'll be teaching your child to appreciate the simple things in life and sending the message that fun doesn't have to cost a fortune.

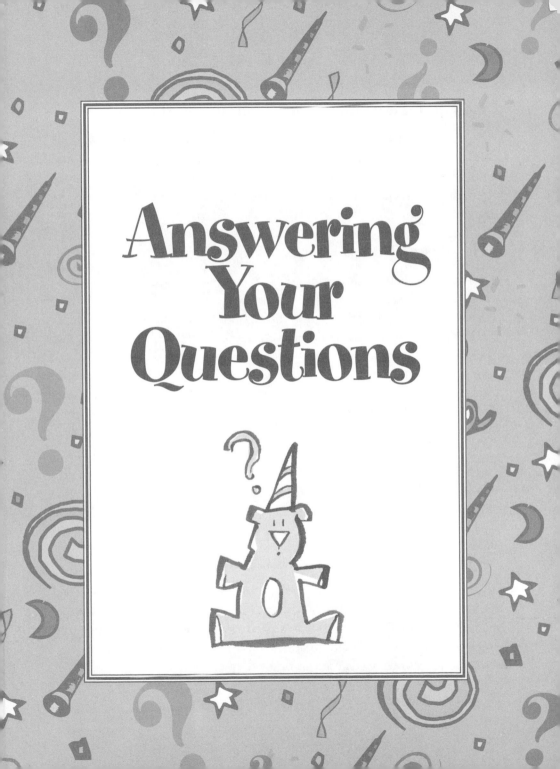

Answering Your Questions

How can I involve my child in the party planning?

First of all, select a party theme together based on the interests of your child. Draw up the invitation list together, and work together to create and send out the invitations. Discuss the party activities with your child, and if your child is old enough, plan them together. Enlist your child's help in the setup for the party.

How do we select a party theme?

A theme is a wonderful way to reflect your child's unique interests and to make the party distinctly his or hers. This book offers fifty party theme ideas, as well as ways to carry the themes throughout the party. To select a theme that's meaningful to your child, ask questions like, "What's your favorite activity? Favorite sport? Favorite book, movie, or television show? What are your special interests? What's your favorite color? Favorite animal? Favorite foods? Favorite games or toys?" Are there any holidays close to your child's birthday? Thinking about these questions and flipping through the themes in this book should provide you with some great ideas.

Once you've selected a theme, make it come alive by incorporating it into several aspects of the party, such as the invitations, the cake, the activities, the decorations, and the party favors. This book will show you how to accomplish this.

Is it really necessary to have a theme party?

A theme is a nice way to tie everything together and make your child feel special. Some parents find that having a theme actually simplifies party-planning because it provides focus. A party doesn't need a theme to be fun, however. Great activities, decorations, cake, and invitations are enjoyed whether or not they're centered around a theme.

Answering Your Questions

How far in advance should we plan the party and send out the invitations?

If you can, start to think about a party theme several weeks before the party. This will give you and your child plenty of time to mull over this decision.

Invitations should go out one to two weeks before the party date. If they're sent out any earlier, guests are likely to forget the date. If they're sent out later, the guests may already have plans for that date.

By the time you send out invitations, you should have at least a rough idea of the decorations, activities, party favors, and cake you'll have at the party. Narrow these decisions down in the days leading up to the party.

Invitations should include an RSVP date. Don't be bashful about calling parents who haven't responded by the RSVP date.

These are the ideal time frames. Some parents enjoy planning their child's party for months in advance. At the other extreme, some parents begin to think about the theme and the party activities the day before the party. The ideas in this book will be helpful no matter where you fall in this spectrum.

How many kids should we invite to the party?

Invite as many as you're comfortable with. The old rule of thumb was one guest for every year of your child's age. For a child turning 4, you'd invite four guests, and for a child turning 6, you'd invite six. Many parents find this guideline unrealistic because their children want to invite many more guests. If you feel you can handle larger parties, then go for it. The new rule of thumb seems to be two guests for every year of your child's age.

The pendulum is swinging toward having bigger, more inclusive birthday parties, especially for children turning 4, 5, 6, and 7. Some schools ask that children invite all of their classmates (especially if invitations are passed out at school), so no one feels left out. If your child's school doesn't request this, you shouldn't feel obligated to invite everyone in your child's class.

It will take a few birthday parties for you to find your comfort zone. Some parents limit their children's parties to eight guests, regardless of age. Others believe that bigger is better, and may allow twenty guests or more. Start small and build up if you're comfortable. Many parents have found ten to twelve guests to be an ideal size.

For older kids, an alternative to large parties is a quiet night to the movies or out to dinner with just two or three close friends. And sleepovers should be small, with no more than five or six guests.

Age	Number of Guests
2	2 to 6
5	3 to 10
4–5	4 to 12
6–8	Up to 14
9–12	Up to 10

How many adults should be present?

You will need at least two adults at your child's party, and even more for large parties. If you're short-handed, consider hiring a neighborhood high-school student to help out at the party, or ask another mother or father for help.

How long should the birthday party run?

One of the most common mistakes is to plan a party that's too long. The party should end on a high note, before little guests get tired or cranky.

Age	Length of Party
2–3	1 to 1.5 hours
4–8	1.5 to 2.5 hours
8–12	1.5 to 3 hours

Some parents swear by a time limit of an hour-and-a-half, regardless of age.

What day and time should we throw the party?

Many parents find that mid-morning and early afternoon parties work best, especially for the younger crowd. If you don't want to serve a meal at the party, the 1–4 P.M. time slot works well because it is after lunch and before dinner.

One of the ways you can add an element of fun to a party, especially for older children, is to throw it at an unusual time. Consider throwing a twilight party, a weekday party, an evening party, or a breakfast party. Of course, you must consider the schedules of your guests when selecting a day and time, such as naps, meals, play groups, school, after-school activities, church, and so on.

What's the most important aspect of a birthday party?

The party games and craft projects—what the kids actually do once they get to the party—are the most important aspects of a birthday party. A snazzy invitation, beautiful decorations, delicious birthday cake, great party favors, and even a nice meal are all impressive elements but by themselves, they don't guarantee a great time. On the other hand, kids can have a blast at the party even if the invitation isn't perfect and even if the decorations aren't amazing. Make the activities your top priority.

What types of activities will work best for my child's age group?

Choosing age-appropriate activities is one of the keys to throwing a great party. The following outline will give you an idea of which types of activities work best for each age. When there's a mix of ages at a party, aim toward the lower end of the age spectrum.

Party Stages

1-year-olds: Party themes for 1-year-olds have not been included in this book because they're generally too young to appreciate a birthday party, and it's difficult to engage 1-year-olds in group activities. First birthdays are usually family celebrations where immediate family and perhaps a few other family members or close friends are invited to a home party.

2-year-olds: Kids this age are curious and like being the center of attention. They like having other children near, but they "parallel play" more than they play interactively. Have a very small party where you will be able to provide some individual attention to each child. Have a simple theme. Include activities such as sing-a-longs, attaching stickers to party hats, and no competitive games. Invite parents. Consider having parties for 2-year-olds in the morning, because many take afternoon naps. Party Suggestions: Ball Party, Music Party.

3-year-olds: Kids this age enjoy exploration of the environment, so be sure to include activities that encourage this, such as an egg hunt or a candy hunt. Other popular activities include sing-a-long games, very easy noncompetitive games, grab bags, moving to music, and simple arts and crafts. Most 3-year-olds like to watch things change, so include activities like watching colored ice cubes melt and "painting" snow. Parents will probably want to stay for this party too. You might consider a morning party for this age group, depending on the napping habits of your child and his or her friends. Party Suggestions: Jungle King Party, Chocolate Factory Party, Dinosaur Party.

4-year-olds: At age 4, kids interact more with each other. They especially like dressing up and hunting for treasures. Most 4-year-olds enjoy playing simple, noncompetitive games. It's also a great age for simple crafts like decorating cupcakes. Party Suggestions: Bug Party, Banana Split Party.

5-year-olds: Team-based activities may be introduced to kids at this age, but try to minimize the competition. They like role-playing, such as playing out the story of Cinderella or pretending to be the family pet, but they're too young for scary activities because they sometimes have trouble separating fantasy from reality. Their little fingers are quite nimble, so crafts are an especially good choice for an activity. This is a good age for a cooking party. Party Suggestions: Pizza Party, Cinderella Party, Young Pajama Party.

6-year-olds: At this age, children are more likely to follow directions and engage in group activities, making the task of running a party easier. Most 6-year-olds are ready for slightly more complex activities, such as treasure hunts using simple or pictorial clues and relay races. Your 6-year-old may prefer to restrict his or her party to the same gender. Party Suggestions: Victorian Tea Party, Mad Scientist Party, Bike Party.

7-year-olds: These kids are excellent listeners, but keep the rules to your games straightforward so they can follow them. They like building things, such as structures out of junk. Kids this age love treasure hunts. Party Suggestions: Architect Party, Olympics Party, Outer Space Party, Rainbow Party.

8-year-olds: You'll find it easier to keep this age group organized around a particular activity. Kids this age are getting sophisticated and enjoy being treated as adults. Activities can go very fast, so consider complex and time-consuming craft projects. Most 8-year-olds like speculating about the future and solving mysteries. Party favors are becoming less important. Party suggestions: Chinatown Party, Starry Night Sleepover Party, Grandmother's Attic Party.

9-year-olds: Because kids this age like lists and classifications, it's a great age for scavenger hunts and treasure hunts based on secret codes. They're also starting to become interested in activities that simulate adult interests. Kids this age will be impressed by something new and different. Sleepover parties may be successful at this age, although some parents prefer to wait until their children are older. Most 9-year-olds also thrive on competition. Party Suggestions: Detective Party, Cloud 9 Party.

10-, 11-, and 12-year-olds: Boys at this age may demand sports parties. At these ages, kids are thinking about the future and also like parties that feel more adult and simulate adult activities. By the time kids reach this age, they are more independent and don't need parents to direct every activity. Parents should expect to play a smaller role in parties of kids this age. Party Suggestions: Glamour Girl Party, Pool Party, Pop Star Party.

What are some sure bets?

There are three things that will work at nearly every party:

Answering Your Questions

- Instant photos are fun for kids of all ages. Consider investing in an instant camera, borrowing one, or purchasing a disposable instant camera for the party. If an instant camera isn't feasible, take photos and send out copies with thank-you notes after the party.

- Music is another important party element. It can play a central role in some activities or be relegated to the background for others. Buy or borrow great music that kids will love. Familiar songs from popular children's movies are always a big hit.

- Treasure hunts are thrilling and are the highlight of many birthday parties. There are variations of treasure hunts for all ages described throughout this book, ranging from simply picking up candy off the ground to hunts with clues in code to elaborate scavenger hunts. Just make sure your treasure hunt is age appropriate.

How do I choose the right mix of activities?

Have a balance of quiet activities and active activities.

Plan an opening activity that works well during the staggered arrivals of the various guests. Arts and crafts work well for this purpose, such as decorating party hats.

Avoid games and activities that may result in problems. Some traditional games can be troublesome, like Musical Chairs and Pin-the-Tail-on-the-Donkey. Substitute modified versions of these games as shown in parties throughout this book. Try to use games that encourage group participation (like relay races), or games that don't result in only one winner.

Don't select games that are too easy or too difficult for the age range of the guests. If there will be much younger or older siblings, then give them a unique role, such as setting up the backyard miniature golf course.

Don't plan competitive games for kids under age 6. Younger kids aren't good losers, and games with winners and losers can result in tears and unpleasant scenes. There are plenty of fun, noncompetitive games recommended throughout the book for younger kids. Some parents avoid competitive games for all ages.

Don't overlook crafts as a fun activity. Games tend to go faster than parents expect, whereas kids can get involved in a fun craft activity for a longer period of time.

What's wrong with games like Musical Chairs and Pin-the-Tail-on-the-Donkey?

Musical Chairs and Simon Says are games of elimination, which means that as the games progress, fewer and fewer children are playing. That leaves a build-up of kids on the sidelines, where they tend to get bored or get into trouble.

Pin-the-Tail-on-the-Donkey is problematic because only one child at a time can play it. That leaves the rest of the guests standing idly by waiting for their turn, which again can lead to boredom and trouble.

Consider a more inclusive version of these games, as shown in the parties throughout this book. For example, 3- and 4-year-olds enjoy an alternative version of musical chairs where a chair is included for each guest on every round; chairs are not eliminated. For older children, play the Circle of Life version of musical chairs, where eliminated children take their chair and start a new circle that grows by one child in each round. When the original circle dwindles down to one child, that child wins a prize, and then the circle of eliminated children becomes the primary circle. Other alternatives to musical chairs are described in this book, such as Pass the Present and Freeze Dance.

At my child's last birthday party, the piñata was very difficult for the kids to break open. In the end, an adult broke it open and tossed the candy around. Is there a better way?

Young children love the anticipation of waiting for a piñata to break open so they can dive for the spilling treats. Parents, on the other hand, sometimes complain that piñatas are too hard to break open and that kids can be ruthless in their quest to grab the goodies that fall out. Some parents are uncomfortable with the subliminal message of violence in an activity that rewards kids for hitting an animal with a stick.

Here are a couple of new options for your next piñata. First of all, you can create a homemade piñata that will be easier to break open and will cost less than store-bought piñatas. Cut the bottom out of a colorful gift bag, and then loosely tape the bottom back in place. Place confetti and goodies inside; decorate the bag with streamers, ribbons, and balloons; tape it closed; and hang it by the handles from your ceiling, a tree, or a swing set. Secondly, if you want to discourage a free-for-all and make the goody distribution more equitable, you can split the goodies into individual bags labeled with names and ask kids to find their bag when the piñata breaks open.

Do I really need to be concerned about what other parents think about the activities or party favors or food we choose for the party?

It's a veritable minefield out there! Some parents think piñatas are violent. Others are upset when toy weapons are given as a party favor. Are all toy weapons off limits, or just guns? What about toy swords? What about squirt guns? Other parents try to restrict the candy and junk food that their children consume and are disappointed when their children receive a goody bag filled with a month's supply of candy. Some parents aren't thrilled by lip gloss and nail polish as party favors, or by dress-up activities that reinforce stereotypical male/female roles. Some are opposed to latex balloons for environmental reasons.

These are just a few of the hot buttons. Should you ban all of these things from your child's party? That's really up to you, but remember that your child's party should be a reflection of his interests. It's important to be aware of the potential concerns that other parents may have, but do what feels right to you.

What's the best sequence for the activities we select?

- Start with an *Icebreaker,* such as a craft project that guests can begin as they arrive, rather than waiting for everyone to get there. It's a nice way for kids who don't know each other to quietly meet before being thrown into games and activities together. It's also a great way for the host to handle the staggered arrival times of guests.

- Move on to one or more *Rev-Up* activities—a relay race, a treasure hunt, or a candy hunt—that pick up the pace and bring some excitement to the party. These will be the more memorable activities for the guests, but they only work if they're timed right.

- Before moving on to cake and presents, plan one or more *Wind-Down* activities—Pass the Present or Tooting to a Jungle Animal Book—to get the kids to calm down. Look for activities that have the kids sitting down.

Answering Your Questions

You'll find that you'll need to be more involved in directing the activities at the beginning of the party. Once the guests have been at the party for a half an hour or so, they'll feel more relaxed and better able to entertain themselves. For this reason, if you plan to have a free play period, consider having it toward the end of the party.

As your children get older, their birthday parties will need less structure and direction from adults. Parties can be more spontaneous. The role of parents eventually evolves to providing the elements for a successful party, and then letting the kids take over.

Is it best to open presents at the end of the party?

There's actually a wide range of opinion on the best way to handle gift opening. First decide whether your birthday child will open gifts at the party or not. Some parents choose to wait until the party is over and the guests have left to open gifts in order to avoid arguments, boredom on the part of the guests, and ungrateful remarks from the birthday child. In parties held outside the home, it is not always practical to open gifts during the party.

Other parents believe that half the fun of giving presents is seeing your gift being opened, so they choose to have their birthday child open gifts at the party for the enjoyment of both the giver and the receiver. A little pre-party coaching on gift opening etiquette can go a long way toward preventing inappropriate reactions, such as ungrateful remarks and the urge to play with the gifts immediately.

If you decide to have your birthday child open gifts during the birthday celebration, it can be handled in a few different ways:

Traditionally, opening gifts is the last party activity.

Some parents let the birthday child open the gifts at the start of the party to relieve present anxiety. The disadvantage of this approach, however, is that it can result in broken toys and lasting distractions.

To make gift opening a more interactive activity, guests can sit on the floor and hold the present they brought on their lap. When the birthday child is ready to open his next gift, the guest stands and brings it up to him.

Gift opening can also be made into a party game. For example, the birthday child can play "Spin the Bottle" or draw names out of a hat to determine whose gift will be opened next.

Take an instant photo of each guest as he or she hands a gift to the birthday child, and let the guests watch the photos develop as the gifts are being opened.

One other alternative for handling presents is to request "no gifts" on the invitation. With so many options, there's sure to be one that's right for you. Choose the approach that you're most comfortable with, and as always, be flexible!

Do you have any guidelines for party favors?

There is a wide range of parental attitudes toward party favors.

- Party favors become less important as children get older, so some parents eliminate them altogether.

- Other parents consider any crafts or projects that the guests create during the party to be the party favor.

- Some parents like to assemble a little goody bag with candy, stickers, and inexpensive toys.

- Some parents prefer to hand out one favor to each guest, such as a small stuffed animal or a picture book that reinforces the party theme.

Involve the birthday child in the party favor decision, and remember that with so many alternatives, you really can't go wrong. For each party theme in the book, there are several suggestions for party favors. Use these ideas as a starting point.

How much time should we allot for each type of activity?

Think about how much time each activity will take, and carefully plan the overall party schedule. For a two-hour party, the basic time guidelines below will work.

Arrival & Icebreaker	20 minutes
Rev-Up Activities	50 to 60 minutes
Wind-Down Activities	15 minutes
Birthday cake and refreshments	10 to 15 minutes
Open Presents	10 to 15 minutes
Party favors, thank you, and goodbye	5 minutes

Given these basic scheduling guidelines and the theme you've chosen, go ahead and construct a rough schedule for the party. Plan the approximate length for each activity, but be prepared for some activities to go much faster than you expected. Others may be such a big hit that kids will want to participate for longer than you expected. Make a plan, but be flexible and have a back-up plan and back-up activities.

How many different structured activities should we plan for the party?

The number of activities you choose for your party is really a reflection of your personal style. Some parents strive to keep the guests engaged as a cohesive group throughout the party and are most comfortable planning a long list of carefully orchestrated games and activities, transitioning to the next game as soon as one is over. These parents may plan six or more structured activities for a two-hour party. (This isn't as impossible as it sounds. You'll see as you review the multitude of ideas for each party theme!) Other parents are more comfortable letting the guests flow from one activity to the next at a slower pace, allowing plenty of time for free play between activities. These parents may plan only two activities for a two-hour party and not worry about losing control over the group. Where's your comfort zone? For most parents, it's somewhere in between these two extremes. It's always a good idea to have a simple game or two in your back pocket, just in case.

What's the best way to decorate for the party?

There are decoration ideas for each of the parties outlined in this book. Fold your own ideas into the mix too. Begin by setting the stage before kids even enter your home by decorating the area outside your home with balloons tied to your mailbox, signs on sticks, streamers on bushes, shapes dangling from trees, sidewalk chalk drawings on the driveway, and decorations on your swing set and fence. Think big. Make it obvious that there's a party there and generate some excitement.

Inside, use simple but festive decorations to create the right atmosphere, such as streamers, balloons, banners, Christmas lights, dangling poster board cut-outs, ribbons hanging in the doorway to the party room, a "throne" for the birthday child, a festive tablecloth, place markers, and confetti sprinkled on the party table. Refer to the theme-specific decorations for each party for more ideas and inspiration. Try to keep the decorations consistent with the theme or within a consistent color scheme, but don't go overboard. Most kids will not notice or appreciate every detail. You may also try to create the feel of a specific location inside the house, such as a jungle or an enchanted forest.

Should we serve a meal?

Younger children are usually satisfied with birthday cake and juice. Kids are so excited during parties that meals often go uneaten. If you do serve a meal to youngsters, keep it very simple, such as peanut butter and jelly sandwiches cut into star shapes.

Serving a meal is more important for older children, but it's still possible to keep it very simple. Pizza is usually a big crowd-pleaser, as well as anything they cook themselves.

What are some of the unpleasant surprises that parents sometimes experience at birthday parties?

Party attendance can be unpredictable. Be prepared for an uninvited guest or two, or some no-shows. You should also be prepared for early and late arrivals.

Have a back-up activity or two in mind (or an area for free play) in case things go much faster than expected.

Expect some poor behavior from the guests or even the birthday child, resulting from the high level of excitement and anticipation.

How do we deal with the problem guest?

A guest who won't participate in the party activities really isn't a problem. Just allow that person to remain on the sidelines as long as he or she is not distracting the others. If, however, a guest disturbs the party with disruptive behavior such as throwing a temper tantrum, crying excessively, or starting a fight, the best way to handle the situation is to remove that guest from the immediate area and try to work out the problem individually. Having more than one adult at the party is necessary to ensure that the party continues to run smoothly while the problem is handled off-line.

What are some strategies to avoid tears or a tantrum from the birthday child?

The guest of honor is likely to be tense with excitement on the party day. Often tantrums or tears result from situations that don't meet the birthday child's expectations, so the best way to avoid problems is to discuss party details ahead of time.

- Decide together which rooms of the house will be off-limits at the party. Put away any toys that will be off-limits.

- Review the guest list with the birthday child, and remind him or her to expect no-shows or late guests.

Answering Your Questions

- Talk about the game plan for the party, focusing on the birthday child's role in each activity.

- Joke about things that could go wrong. What if Mom drops the cake? What if the birthday child spills punch? Make light of these potential disasters, point out the humor in them, and decide what course of action you'd take to remedy the situation. That way, when something unexpected happens, the birthday child will be able to handle it.

- Talk about sharing, winning and losing, and the importance of being a good sport, even if you aren't planning competitive games.

- Review the list of the party activities together.

- Coach your birthday child on reacting politely and enthusiastically when opening gifts.

How can I prevent the group of partygoers from getting out-of-control?

Avoiding idle time is the best way to prevent out-of-control group behavior. Aim to keep the partygoers busy and entertained throughout the party. Prepare as much as you can beforehand—labeling, slicing, pouring, scooping, setting up—so the action doesn't have to stop while you prepare something.

Keeping the entire group of partygoers engaged in the same activity at the same time is nearly impossible at parties for 2- and 3-year-olds. Control becomes easier to achieve as the kids get older. Expect some younger kids to refuse to participate in some activities and to be easily distracted.

Any suggestions for making the birthday child feel extra special?

Personalize Make the birthday child feel special by customizing as many things as possible, such as decorations (a "Happy Birthday, Bonnie!" banner, or her name spelled out in jelly beans). Make a special birthday hat for the birthday child to wear year after year, decorated with a feather or a ring of colorful pom-poms around the bottom and glitter-glue writing (with a saying such as "Birthday Girl" or "Happy Birthday, Audrey!"). Create a personalized birthday party tablecloth to use every year by stamping your child's handprints with glittery fabric paint. Decorate a chair as the throne for the birthday child. The birthday child will sit on the throne when "Happy Birthday" is sung and while opening presents.

Beautiful Baby Put a framed photo of the birthday child as a baby on the table.

Surprise Although the birthday child will be involved in the party planning, keep some details secret. A child will be delighted with a surprise or two at the party.

Let The Birthday Child Be First When you play games in which one child is "it," start with the birthday child being "it." When an activity requires that kids take turns, let the birthday child go first, like making the first strike at the piñata. Serve the birthday child the first piece of birthday cake, the first cup of juice, and so on.

Make Lasting Memories Take lots of photos or videos. Send extra copies of photos with thank-you cards. Have a party sign-in sheet or an autograph book.

Answering Your Questions

Are thank-you notes necessary?

Sending thank-you notes is an appropriate gesture of gratitude, although some parents don't consider them to be an absolute must. Sending thank-you notes helps children develop good manners at a young age. It's also a way to continue the fun using the party's theme. Some parents don't let their kids play with their birthday gifts until thank-you notes have been sent to the givers. If gifts were not opened at the party, sending a thank-you note is even more important.

Consider sending photocopied artwork as a thank-you or a computer-generated thank-you. Enclose a photo from the party.

How should we plan a party for twins?

It isn't necessary to have two separate parties for twins. The siblings can work together to plan one party that represents both their interests, because twins often have common friends. Within the one party, you may have two distinctly different themes. You can conduct a couple of activities around each theme, and even decorate half of the room (or half of the party table) in one theme, and half in the other theme. Make sure you have two different birthday cakes, sing Happy Birthday twice, and have the kids open their presents separately.

You can also schedule separate times to make the party actually two parties in one. For example, devote the first hour to one twin, and the second hour to the other twin.

As the twins become old enough for parties outside the home, another alternative is to throw two parties that become one. For example, Mom can take one twin and her friends to one destination (a bowling alley, for example), while Dad takes the other twin and her friends to another destination (a beauty salon, for example). Then all the kids from both parties get together at a common destination like a pizza parlor or back home for cake and opening presents.

My daughter wants a sleepover party, but I think she's too young. When are kids ready for sleepovers?

Some parents have had successful sleepover parties for 8-year-olds, while others prefer to wait until their child is 10, 11, or 12. The right age varies widely from one child to the next and from one geographic area to another. Talk to other parents, and do what seems best for you.

If your child is too young for a sleepover party but is still enthralled with the idea of one, consider the Young Pajama Party. Guests come dressed in their pajamas, play sleepover-type games, and then go home before actually going to bed.

Sleepovers should be same-sex parties only. Start with an active period, where the kids can play active games, have a Treasure Hunt, or even go out bowling or roller-skating. Beauty makeovers are also popular at sleepovers. Serve something fun to eat, like pizza, then wind down with a rented movie. Storytelling is a fun activity just before bed.

For a sleepover party to be successful, it needs to have the right blend of spontaneous activity and structured activity. Focus on providing the elements for fun, and then give the children some independence in directing their own activities. Refer to some of the specific themes in the book for more ideas.

Answering Your Questions

What can we do to prevent safety accidents at the party?

Balloons are a choking hazard and bad for the environment. If you have young children at the party, use Mylar balloons instead of latex, keep the balloons out of reach, or forget balloons altogether.

Ban the family dog. Some kids are afraid of dogs, and even the gentlest animals can be unpredictable and excitable when there are several kids around.

Carefully select foods that aren't a choking hazard, especially for the younger crowd. For example, whole grapes, hot dogs, hard candies, peanuts, and popcorn shouldn't be served to toddlers.

A piñata is great fun for the kids, but it can easily get out of control. Manage it by requiring kids to wait in a line that's far back from the swinging bat or pole.

What can the birthday child learn from his or her party?

A birthday party is a wonderful opportunity to teach your child some important life lessons. For example, you can teach your child:

- to consider the feelings of others when setting the guest list, handing out invitations, and opening gifts.

- that good manners make guests feel comfortable and relaxed. Have your child help you make introductions among guests who don't know each other, greet arriving guests with enthusiasm, and thank departing guests.

- to be tolerant of others. Not every guest will be eager to dive into every activity.

- to be flexible. Prepare your child to expect the unexpected, and to not get upset when it happens!

- that the simple things in life, like spending time with friends, are the best and don't need to be expensive.

- that a little bit of creativity goes a long way.

- that he or she is valued and loved. Working together on a joint project like a birthday party deepens the parent-child relationship and builds lasting memories.

How to use this book

Each party outlined in this book has suggestions for:

- Invitations

  The suggestions for handmade invitations are simple ideas that can be quickly created at home with minimal fuss. The birthday child often enjoys the process of creating the invitations. You may also consider invitations made on a home computer. If you're pressed for time, store-bought or mail-order invitations are available for many themes. Even if you don't make the invitations, the birthday child can still add a personal touch by decorating the outside of the envelope with stickers, doodles, or hand outlines. The best invitations generate excitement and enthusiasm for the party.

- Activities

  For many parties, there are more activities described than you'll have time for. This enables you to select the ones that are most appealing to the birthday child and to have a backup activity in case one finishes up earlier than you expected.

- Decorations

  In addition to the suggestions throughout the book, a visit to a party goods store or flipping through a birthday supply catalog may give you more ideas.

- Cake

  The cake ideas are simple and can be made at home using a mix. If you'd rather call in a professional, you can visit your local bakery or supermarket with an idea to see if they can make it for you, or add a unique decoration to the top of a store-bought cake. Another source to consider for cakes is ice cream stores, such as Friendly's and Baskin Robbins, which sell several different theme cakes.

- **Party Favors**

    There are long lists of possibilities for party favors for each theme, more ideas than you'll need. Pick and choose the ones that sound the most fun or are the most available. You don't need to spend a fortune on party favors. Just give items that are cheerful, fun, festive, colorful, and if possible, reinforce the party theme. A great source for party favors is the Oriental Trading Company (1-800-228-2269, oriental.com), which sells inexpensive party favors through a mail-order catalog and online.

Mix it up!

If you'd like to, mix things up! Pick and choose activities from different themes that sound like fun, modifying them to the theme of your party. Use the ideas in this book as a source for inspiration!

To theme or not to theme

A theme isn't absolutely necessary. If you like some of the ideas but don't want a theme party, then go ahead and use the ideas without a theme. You can use this book to get ideas for activities.

The themes are adaptable. If your child has his heart set on a theme revolving around the hero in the latest hit children's movie, but that theme isn't in this book, then you can use this book to find a similar theme and adapt it. For example, the Outer Space Party can be adapted depending on the space movie, television show, or character that's the latest rage. If your

7-year-old loves the idea of a Detective Party but the Detective Party in this book sounds too old, then simplify the ideas and borrow from other parties to target the right age range.

Age appropriateness

Use your judgment. The parties all have recommendations on appropriate ages, but these are merely guidelines and may be adjusted depending on your individual situation.

Parties for Young Children

Noah's Ark Party

*The rain, the animal pairs, and the ark are all
part of this wonderful celebration for youngsters.*

Ages: 2 to 4

Invitations

Cut a boat shape out of construction paper and glue it to the outside of a folded piece of heavyweight paper. Let the birthday child add animal stickers to the scene. Write "Climb Aboard Kristen's Ark to Celebrate Her Third Birthday!" on the outside and list the party details inside. Ask guests to bring a small stuffed animal to join them on the ark. Decorate the outside of the envelope with raindrops.

Activities

Animal Ark As guests arrive, ask them to place their stuffed animals in the ark so they can watch the party. You can use a toy boat, a large basket, or an inverted open umbrella for the ark.

Noah's Ark Party

Animal Passports Guests each create a passport booklet for their travels. Create the booklets before the party by photocopying a real passport cover onto heavyweight colored papers, cutting them down to size, folding them in half, punching a hole at the top, and threading a piece of yarn through them so the guests can wear their passports around their necks. Write each guest's name on the cover of a passport and let guests decorate their covers with markers and crayons. Provide non-toxic stamp pads and ask the partygoers to stamp a fingerprint inside their passport. Throughout the party, the children will win animal stickers to place inside their passports. Start this process by handing the guests each an animal sticker as they complete their animal passports.

Duck Pond Before the party, gather several rubber ducks, so you'll have one for each guest. Write a number in permanent marker on the underside of each duck. Gather several party favors, wrap them, and label them with numbers that correspond to the numbers on the ducks. At the party, float the ducks in a large basin of water. Let each guest reach in, select a duck, turn it over, and read the number. Then let him locate the corresponding party favor and open it. Add a sticker to his animal passport.

Animal Pairs Before the party, get several pairs of toy animal figurines, so there's one pair for each partygoer. Hide one animal in the party room and place the other animal in a bowl. At the party, let each child pick an animal out of the bowl and then try to find its mate. Make this game more challenging for 4- and 5-year-olds by hiding the mates in harder-to-find places and drawing a picture of the hiding place on an index card that's taped to the first animal. The children use these clues to find the matching animals. Once they have a matching pair, the guests turn them in to earn another animal sticker for their passports.

Cookie Painting Before the party, make or buy sugar cookie dough. Roll out a section for each child. At the party, the kids cut the cookie dough into animal shapes using several different cookie cutters, and then an adult bakes the cookies. Move on to the next activity while the cookies are baking and cooling. (In parties for 2- and 3-year-old children, you may want to skip this first step and go right to decorating pre-made cookies.) Once the cookies are cool, the children can paint decorations onto them. Mix two egg whites with a teaspoon of water and divide the mixture into several cupcake tins. (Some grocery stores sell pasteurized egg whites.) Add food coloring to each one. The kids use clean paintbrushes to paint the animal cookies. Give the guests a passport sticker for each cookie they paint.

Huckle Buckle Beanstalk The birthday child shows his guests the stuffed animal that he placed in the ark at the beginning of the party. He hides this animal in the party room while all the guests are waiting in another room. He must hide it in a location that is visible without moving anything in the room. Once the animal is hidden, the birthday child calls the guests back into the party room. The first guest to spot the hidden animal yells, "Huckle Buckle Beanstalk!" and then it's that guest's turn to hide his animal on the next round. Give an animal sticker to the guest who finds the hidden animal on each round. Continue playing for several rounds.

Duck Pond Gift Opening When it's time to open the gifts, recycle the rubber duck setup. Number each gift with a slip of paper and let the guests hold their gifts in their laps while they sit on the floor in a circle. Let the birthday child draw a duck from the pond and announce the number. The guest with that number on her gift hands the gift to the birthday child to open, and the guest wins an animal sticker to add to her passport. Continue until all the gifts have been opened.

Decorations

Cut raindrop shapes out of blue cellophane and tape them to the windows. Decorate the party table with an assortment of toy boats and pairs of animal figurines.

Cake

Bake a round layer cake and frost it with blue frosting. Place a toy boat on top of the cake along with a pair of animal figurines. Circle several other pairs of animal figurines around the base of the cake.

Party Favors

Animal stickers
Painted animal cookies
Animal crackers
Animal coloring books
Animal figurines

Music Party

*Your young child will love sharing his or her love
for music, marching, and dancing with friends.*
Ages: 2 to 4

Invitations

Make a CD invitation by spray painting a circle of construction paper with metallic silver paint, punching a hole in the center, and using a permanent marker to write, "You're Invited to Shake, Rattle, and Roll at Michael's Musical Birthday Party!" in block letters. Write the party details on the plain back.

Activities

Making Maracas Kids create maracas out of household objects. Put out a selection of containers such as margarine tubs, coffee cans, jars, and plastic bottles. You may spray paint them ahead of time to make them colorful. For the noisy fillings, fill bowls with dried peas, rice, beans, dry pasta, sand, pebbles, and rocks. As guests arrive, let them each select a container, fill it, and then decorate it with stickers and markers.

Story Shake The kids sit on the floor in a circle as an adult reads a popular children's book. Select a magic word that's repeated throughout the story, such as the title character's name, and tell the kids that every time they hear the magic word, they should shake their maracas. In the second round, hand out kazoos or noisemakers and have kids blow these every time they hear the magic word. At parties for older children, have a third round, where there are two magic words, one for maracas and one for kazoos. The kids will enjoy the challenge of trying to remember which instrument to play when.

Freeze Dance Play familiar children's music and let the kids shake their maracas as they dance to the music. When the music stops, everyone must freeze in place for as long as they can.

Sing-a-long Sing and dance to a couple of familiar action songs, such as "Ring around the Rosie," "London Bridge," "If You're Happy and You Know It," "I'm a Little Teapot," "Teddy Bear Teddy Bear," and "Hokey Pokey."

Musical Chairs Set up for musical chairs using the same number of chairs as guests. As music plays, the guests walk around the chairs. When the music stops, they scurry to sit down in a chair. Cheer, and then play several more rounds. No need to eliminate chairs for this young crowd.

Music Parade The guests wear birthday hats, tie jingle bells to their shoes, and march to music as they play their maracas or kazoos.

Name That Tune Kids sit on the floor in a circle while you play children's music. Ask them to shout out the name of the song as soon as they recognize it. Cheer enthusiastically when someone correctly identifies the song, and then reward all of them with a party favor at the end of the game.

Decorations

Play kids' tunes outside to welcome guests to the music party. Decorate inside with real musical instruments if you have any. Miniature musical instruments are available as Christmas ornaments and look festive hanging from the lighting fixture or at the entrance to the party room. You may also thread pieces of ribbon through the center of CDs and dangle these from above. Don't forget a musical noisemaker, such as a kazoo, at each place setting.

Cake

Make a drum cake by using small, round cake pans and stacking three cakes, or make a double batch of cake batter and stack four normal-sized round cakes. Draw a zigzag design on the side of the cake with frosting. Use two long, thin breadsticks as edible drumsticks and perch them on top of the cake.

Party Favors

Toy instruments
Miniature notepads with a musical motif
Music stickers
Kazoos
Harmonicas
Bells
Noisemakers

Happy Face Party

*Many young children love the universal happy face and will be delighted
to have this festive icon serve as the central theme of their celebration.*

Ages: 2 to 4

Invitations

Cut a circle out of yellow paper and use a black marker to draw a happy
face on it. Write the party details in short phrases that stretch around the
outside border of the face.

Activities

Party Hat Decorating Purchase solid-colored hats and put these out
along with happy face stickers. As guests arrive, invite them to decorate their
party hats with stickers.

Happy Face Decorating Before the party, cut clear contact paper and a piece of yellow construction paper into 8 inch (8") circles (approximately). Tape the clear contact paper down to the table with the sticky side facing up. Lay out small shapes of colorful paper and sparkly confetti on paper plates. Encourage the guests to sprinkle the colored paper and confetti onto their sticky contact paper. They may create a happy face design on the contact paper, or it may be a more free-form design. Once they're through decorating their contact paper, help them stick their large yellow circles of paper to the contact paper to seal their decorations in place.

Happy Face Tattoos and Face Paint As guests complete their party hats, ask if they would like a temporary tattoo placed on their arm or a happy face painted on their cheek using face paint.

Happy Sing-a-long Lead the guests in a group sing-a-long of "If You're Happy and You Know It" followed by other favorites of the birthday child, such as "Hokey Pokey" or "Old MacDonald."

Happy Face Pizzas Pre-cook individual-sized round pizza dough crusts. You may use store-bought pizza dough for this. At the party, lay these out along with pizza ingredients—tomato sauce, cheese, green peppers, mushrooms, and pepperoni. Encourage the guests to create their own pizzas. They may even create a happy face pizza using pepperoni for the eyes and green pepper for the mouth.

Happy Face Lollipop Hunt Before the party, purchase happy face lollipops (or create them by using a permanent marker to draw a happy face on the clear wrapper of flat lollipops). Hide the lollipops in a designated area and encourage the party guests to gather as many as they can.

Happy Face Party

Happy Ballooney Decorate a yellow balloon with a happy face using a black permanent marker. The guests stand in a circle and hit the balloon in the air, trying to keep it from touching the ground.

Decorations

Use solid yellow as the color for streamers, paper goods, and wrapping paper. Buy a bouquet of yellow helium balloons and draw happy faces on them. Draw happy faces outside using sidewalk chalk, and dangle yellow poster-board happy faces from lamps or trees throughout the party room or yard.

Cake

Serve cupcakes decorated with yellow frosting. Guests can add black or brown candies to create a happy face on their cupcakes.

Party Favors

Happy face stickers
Yellow balls with happy faces drawn in black permanent marker
Happy face paper and pencils
Happy face squeeze toys
Happy face lollipops
Happy face balloons
Yellow sand pails with happy faces drawn in black permanent marker

Construction Party

For little tykes fascinated by trucks, dirt, and driving, this party will be paradise!
Ages: 2 to 5

Invitations

Cut a traffic sign shape out of colored paper. Write "Drive on Over to Andrew's Construction Birthday Party!" on the front in block letters and outline the party details on the back. Ask the guests to bring their favorite truck to the party.

Activities

Free Truck Play As the kids arrive, let them play with their trucks in a sandbox or in a pile of dirt or sand.

Truck Driver's License The kids create their own truck driver's license so they will be eligible to drive through the obstacle course. Lay out index cards, pictures of trucks and truck logos from magazines, truck stickers, glue sticks, and markers, and let the kids create their own truck driver's license. Laminate these with clear contact paper.

Truck Driver's Obstacle Course Set up an obstacle course for the kids' trucks to run through. Include obstacles such as ramps, piles of dirt, and holes. You can set up the obstacle course before the party or involve the kids in setting up the obstacle course at the party. The kids run their trucks through the course, and they all win a small party favor.

Truck Running Race Line the guests up behind a starting line, and place the trucks that the kids brought on a finish line that's several feet away. At "Go!" the guests run to the finish line, find their trucks, bring them back to the starting line, and place them on the ground. Then they run back to the finish line to collect a party favor. At parties for younger children, modify this game by having them simply race to find their truck on the finish line.

Truckle Buckle Beanstalk Get a small construction vehicle (the size of a child's fist or smaller) and show it to all the kids. The birthday child then hides the truck somewhere in a room while the guests wait in another room. The hidden truck must be visible without moving anything in the room. The waiting kids are called in once the truck is hidden, and with their hands behind their backs, they walk around the room looking for the hidden truck. As soon as a guest spots it, he yells "Truckle Buckle Beanstalk!" Then that guest hides the truck while the others wait in another room, and another round of the game is played. Continue playing for several rounds.

Truck Stop and Go (ages 4 and up) Before the party, draw a racetrack on the driveway using sidewalk chalk. It should contain a separate lane for each guest and truck. Draw eight lines across the racetrack, so that there are eight squares in each truck's lane. Also, prepare a dozen or so slips of paper with a number on each one: 1, 2, or 3. At the party, the kids line up their trucks at the starting line, and each guest draws a slip of paper from a bowl and moves his truck forward by the number of spaces indicated on the slip of paper. Then the kids return the slips of paper to the bowl and draw again. Continue playing until all the guests have crossed the finish line, and give each guest a prize as he makes it.

Red Light, Green Light (ages 4 and up) The guests line up behind the starting line. The birthday child stands with his back to the group at the finish line. As he yells, "green light, green light, green light," several times, the guests can move their trucks forward toward the finish line. When he yells "red light!" he turns around and faces the guests, who must freeze in place when they hear "red light!" If he spots any trucks being moved, those guests and their trucks must go back to the starting line. Then the birthday child can resume calling, "green light, green light." The first guest to reach the finish line takes the birthday child's place in the next round.

Decorations

Hang construction and traffic signs made from poster board. Decorate with bright yellow streamers (see if you can find streamers labeled "construction") and bright orange cones. Add colorful blinking Christmas lights.

Cake

Start with a sheet cake, and using crushed Oreo's, brown sugar, and mocha frosting, create a construction site with mounds of dirt and dirt paths. Put a couple of miniature trucks on top of the cake.

Party Favors

Miniature trucks
Truck stickers and traffic stickers
Truck driver's licenses
Key chains

Jungle King Party

Youngsters will enjoy this wild safari party with a wide variety of quiet and active games. If you have a zoo or animal park nearby, you may consider holding this party there.

Ages: 2 to 6

Invitations

Cut colored paper or wrapping paper into the shape of a jungle animal, such as an elephant, a lion, or a zebra. To get a shape outline, trace a shape from a book or use cookie cutters. Glue the animal shape to the outside of a piece of folded heavyweight paper. Write "Get Wild at Benjamin's Jungle King Birthday Party!" on the outside and write the party details inside. Ask guests to bring a small stuffed animal to the party.

Activities

Jungle Mural Hang a roll of wide white paper along one or two walls of the party room. Get some jungle wrapping paper and cut out a few dozen animals and plants. Use a glue stick to attach some jungle plants and trees to the mural paper. As the guests arrive at the party, give them a glue stick and some animal cutouts and let them add to the jungle scene.

Jungle Cookies Before the party, bake animal-shaped sugar cookies using animal cookie cutters and a roll of pre-made cookie dough or dough that you make from scratch. For the cookie paint, mix two egg whites with a teaspoon of water. (Some grocery stores sell pasteurized egg whites.) Divide the mixture into several cupcake tins, and add different food coloring to each one. At the party, give the guests clean paintbrushes then let them paint the animal cookies with stripes and polka dots.

Animal Parade Paint kids' faces to look like jungle animals, such as a zebra, a lion, or a leopard. Get some non-toxic inkpads and stamp animals onto kids' hands, or apply temporary tattoos. Then conduct an animal parade in the yard. Play jungle music and have the kids carry their stuffed animals while they march around the yard behind the birthday child who is holding a stick (a yardstick or dowel) with streamers attached. At the end of the parade, present homemade award ribbons to all of the stuffed animals for the furriest, largest, most colorful, longest hair, smallest, and most scary.

Lion, Lion, Tiger (ages 4 and up) Play this game like Duck, Duck, Goose. Kids sit in a circle on the floor. The child who is "it" walks around the outside of the circle in a clockwise direction, tapping each child's head as he says the name of an animal, either "Lion" or "Tiger." He starts by saying "Lion" several times—as many times as he wants to—but the first time that he says

"Tiger," the seated child who received the accompanying tap jumps up, runs around the circle, and tries to make it back to her spot. At the same time, the child who was "it" runs around the circle and tries to beat her. Whoever sits in the vacated spot first can keep that spot. The remaining child is "it" and walks around the circle saying "Lion," "Lion," etc., "Tiger" again. Younger children who are unfamiliar with this game will need coaching from an adult.

Jungle Mix-Up (ages 4 and up) Establish a starting line and a finish line several yards away from each other. Each guest is assigned a jungle animal by drawing stickers or names out of a bowl. Players must stand behind the starting line to be "safe." An adult stands between the starting line and the finish line and calls out animal names one by one. As each animal is called out, the kids assigned that animal must race to the finish line and cross it without being tagged by the adult. Any kids who are tagged become helpers and try to tag other kids as they run by. When the adult yells, "All Jungle Animals!" then all remaining players behind the starting line must race to the finish line. Continue playing several rounds.

Jungle Safari Before the party, put each guest's party favors into a separate plastic storage box such as an empty diaper wipe box or an index card box. Attach a sticker of a jungle animal to the box, and then tie a piece of ribbon around the box. Attach matching stickers to a set of index cards. If possible, try to get as many different animal stickers as there are guests at the party. Hide the treasure boxes in one area of the yard, perhaps camouflaged by leaves, sticks, or bushes. Hide the index cards in a different area of the house or yard. At the party, hand out safari helmets for the guests to wear, and explain they're going on a safari to find rare jungle animals in your yard. First, each guest must find one animal card. Then he must find the treasure box with a sticker that matches the sticker on the animal card. Once all the guests find their boxes, they can present them to an adult to check the matching animals and cut the ribbon. Make this game a little simpler for 3-year-olds by placing the party favor boxes in conspicuous hiding spots and letting the children each pull an animal index card out of a bowl to determine which animal they'll hunt for. For 2-year-olds, scatter animal stickers, candies, or figurines in an area of the house or yard and let the kids scurry to pick up as many as they can.

Jungle Tag Designate an area, such as a driveway or a corner of your backyard, for the game. Identify one or two guests to be the lions (you should have roughly one lion for every six guests). The other guests, the zebras, try to avoid being tagged by the lions. If a zebra is tagged, he must stand frozen in place. An unfrozen zebra may thaw the frozen zebra by crawling on his belly through the zebra's legs. Once a zebra has been frozen three times, he becomes a lion and helps tag the other zebras.

Huckle Buckle Beanstalk Play this game with the stuffed animals that the kids brought. Start with the birthday child, who shows the guests his stuffed animal and then hides the animal somewhere in a room while the guests wait in another room. The hidden animal must be visible without moving any objects in the room. The waiting kids are called into the room once the animal is hidden, and with their hands behind their backs, they walk around the room looking for the hidden animal. As soon as someone spots it, he yells "Huckle Buckle Beanstalk!" Then that guest hides his stuffed animal while the others wait in another room. Play several rounds.

Animal Pantomime The child who is "it" acts out the movements of an animal without making any sounds. The child who correctly identifies the animal being portrayed becomes "it" and selects another animal to act out. Animal suggestions include snake, frog, bird, fish, turtle, monkey, rabbit, dog, bear, squirrel, mouse, cat, and bug. For 3- and 4-year-olds, you can place a collection of animal stickers in a bowl and let guests draw a sticker out of the bowl to determine which animal they'll act out. At parties of 2- and 3-year-olds, an adult can yell out animal names and have all the children join in acting out the animal movements.

Jungle Relay Race (ages 5 and up) Split the kids into two teams. Establish a starting line, and place the stuffed animals that the kids brought with them in a pile or in a laundry basket several feet from the starting line. The first child in each line must run to the pile of stuffed animals, rescue his animal, and bring it back to his line. Once he slaps the hand of the next child in line, that guest runs to the pile, finds his stuffed animal, and brings it back. The first team to rescue all of its stuffed animals wins.

Animal Toot (ages 2 to 4) Give each guest a noisemaker or an inexpensive plastic whistle. The kids sit on the floor in a circle and listen to an adult read a book about a jungle animal. Instruct the kids that every time they hear the title character's name, they should toot their whistle or noisemaker.

Zoo House If you live near a zoo, an animal park, or a farm, find out if they'll bring a few small animals to your party for the kids to pet and learn about; or, consider holding your party at the zoo. Some of the games described in this birthday party may be played at your zoo, such as Lion, Lion, Tiger; Jungle Safari; Jungle Relay Race; and Animal Pantomime. You may want to give guests a sticker book for a party favor and hand out stickers at each animal stop.

Decorations

Decorate with animal prints, using items such as zebra striped crepe paper, a leopard spotted tablecloth, and tiger striped balloons. Add plants, bird ornaments, and fake ivy.

Have the kids wear safari helmets instead of birthday hats.

Cake

Create a jungle scene on top of a sheet cake by placing animal figurines on a green background. Have the kids place their stuffed animals in a cage (under an inverted laundry basket or in a wire animal crate) to watch their owners eat cake.

Party Favors

Place the party favors in the center of a square of animal-print fabric, then wrap the fabric around the favors and tie a ribbon around the top, sack-style.

Sticker albums and animal stickers
Small plastic animal figures
Animal print Band-Aids
Animal crackers
Safari helmets
Animal candy—gummy bears or red licorice fish
Whistles
Animal capsules (expand into sponges when immersed in water)

Kittens and Puppies Party

Fantasy play comes alive at this party, where guests are transformed into adorable little kittens and puppies.

Ages: 2 to 6

Invitations

Create a two-sided invitation with a puppy face on one side and a kitten face on the other. Cut heavyweight colored paper into the shape of a round face. On one side, draw pointy kitten ears, kitten eyes, a triangular nose, and whiskers. Write, "Meow! Woof! You're Invited to Justin's Kittens and Puppies Party!" under the kitten nose. On the other side, draw puppy eyes and eyebrows at the top and long puppy ears down the sides. Write the party details in the center, under the puppy eyes. You can enhance your drawings by gluing on wiggly eyes and by using fake fur for the kitten ears and puppy eyebrows. Create a track of paw prints across the outside of the envelope by using a stamp pad or by drawing them with a marker.

Activities

Kitty and Puppy Visitors If you or a friend have a kitten or a puppy that is friendly with children, invite the pet to the party and let the children pet it as they arrive.

Edible Pet Collars The partygoers create cat collars by stringing Froot Loops, Lifesavers, pasta wheels, and other foods with a hole onto a thin strand of licorice or yarn.

Kitten and Puppy Dress-Up Transform the children into adorable kittens or puppies using face paint. Clip on furry ears using bobby pins, barrettes, or a headband and let the children wear the collars they created. Ask each child to select a pet name and write the name on a party favor bag along with the child's human name. Add a kitten or puppy tattoo. Take instant photos of the pets!

Kitty and Puppy Dancing Play some lively music while the kittens dance and scamper and meow, and the puppies bark and dance on all fours. When the music stops, the pets must freeze in place. Play several rounds.

Kitten and Puppy Treasure Hunt Before the party, gather a few dozen fish-shaped cat treats and bone-shaped dog treats. Bury them in a large sandbox. The guests all line up around the sandbox, and when an adult says, "Go!" they all dig to find treats. The guests dressed as puppies try to find bones, and the guests dressed as kittens try to find fish. They can turn in each pet treat for a human treat at the end of the dig. At parties for older children, you may hide the treats in a large area rather than bury them in a sandbox and send the puppies and kittens to hunt for them.

Puppy, Puppy, Who Has the Bone? In the first round, the birthday child is the puppy and is sent to sit in a chair with her back to the other children while a bone is placed on the floor behind the puppy's chair. Meanwhile, the other children sit on the floor in a circle and pass a ball while music is played. When the music stops, the child holding the ball sneaks to the chair, takes the puppy's bone, returns to the circle, and hides the bone under his legs. The circle of children then chants, "Puppy, Puppy, Who Has the Bone?" The puppy faces the circle and has three guesses to identify the child who took the bone. The child who took the bone becomes the puppy in the next round. This game can also be modified to "Kitty, Kitty, Who Has the Fish?"

Blind Kitty Buff (ages 4 and up) Blindfold the guest who's "it," and turn him around three times. The other guests make kitty meowing and purring sounds while the child who is "it" tries to tag them. The first person tagged becomes "it" next. On the next round, the guests make puppy barking, growling, and howling sounds. Play several rounds of this game in a safe, open area.

Kitten and Puppy Relay Race (ages 4 and up) Divide guests into two teams: the kittens and the puppies. Give each team a large spoon and a bowl. Place a bag of dog food opposite the puppies' line and a bag of cat food opposite the kittens' line. One at a time, team members run with the spoon to the bag of food, pick up a spoonful, run back to the team's bowl, and drop the food into the bowl. At the end, compare the amount of food that each team has transferred into their bowls. Play several rounds with variations such as running backwards, stepping sideways, having the teammates bark and meow, and so on. Award small prizes to the members of the winning team and consolation prizes to the other team.

Decorations

The birthday child will enjoy creating a dog house and a cat house before the party by decorating large appliance boxes from which an adult has cut doorways. Decorate the party table with stuffed cats and dogs. If you have an animal crate, some stuffed animals can watch the party fun from inside it. Create bone-shaped and fish-shaped place cards for the table and decorate the party hats with paw prints (using a marker, ink pad, or stickers).

Cake

Decorate individual cupcakes with kitten and puppy faces. Frost the cupcakes, then cut fruit roll-ups into triangle-shaped kitten ears or long puppy ears. Add black licorice strings for kitten whiskers, jelly beans for eyes, flat round or triangular candies for the noses, and a half-buried red lollipop for puppy tongues.

Party Favors

Red licorice fish
Instant Photos of each guest dressed up as a pet
Small stuffed kittens or puppies
Kitten or puppy figurines
Kitten and puppy stickers
Pet collars
Miniature Kit Kat candy bars

Dinosaur Party

This party is serious fun for dinosaur fanatics and their friends!
Ages: 2 to 7

Invitations

Cut green paper into the shape of a dinosaur using a cookie cutter or by tracing a shape from a book. Write "Come to Alex-saurus Rex's Dinosaur Birthday Party!" on the body. Outline the shape with glitter glue and write the party details on the back. Add, "Come Have a Roaring Good Time!" to the back.

Activities

Dinosaur Creatures Cut large dinosaur shapes from heavyweight white art paper. Cut several colors of tissue paper into 1 inch (1") squares and lay these out on a table along with small paintbrushes and miniature condiment cups filled with a mixture of half glue and half water. The guests create colorful dinosaurs by painting them with glue and attaching the tissue paper.

Dinosaur Egg Hunt Place small party favors or candies inside a few dozen plastic eggs. Scatter the dinosaur eggs around an area of your house or yard. Give each guest a bag and let them race to pick up as many eggs as they can. To make this more challenging for older children, hide the eggs and draw picture clues hinting at their locations.

Dinosaur Walk Before the party, arrange several paper plates in a circle, about one footstep apart. There should be as many paper plates as participants. Write a number on each paper plate and tape it to the ground or floor. At the party, play peppy music as the guests walk around the circle, stepping from plate to plate. When the music stops, the children each stand on a numbered plate, and an adult pulls a number from a bowl. The child standing on the plate with the number called wins a prize. Keep playing until every guest has won at least one prize. To make things move faster, you can draw two numbers from the bowl on each round. At parties for 2- and 3-year-olds, you may want to make each plate a different color rather than numbering them.

Prehistoric Obstacle Course Create an obstacle course for the participants using chairs to run around, broomsticks to crawl under, trampolines or pillows to bounce on, piles of blocks to jump over, and so on. Set up a cave at the beginning of the obstacle course using sheets and chairs, and place several dinosaur figurines inside the tent. At the end of the obstacle course, place some leaves in a laundry basket. At the party, tell the guests that some hungry dinosaurs are hiding in the Dinosaur Cave. Demonstrate how the children must go into the cave, retrieve a dinosaur, help it through the entire obstacle course, and at the end toss the dinosaur into the basket filled with leaves so it can eat lunch. Reward each runner with a gold chocolate coin medal at the end of the obstacle course. You may also hand out awards for successful completion of the obstacle course to the "Super Jumper," "Super Runner," "Super Dinosaur Kicker," and "Super Bouncer."

Dinosaur Dig Bury several bone-shaped dog biscuits in the birthday child's sandbox. Tell the children that many years ago, dinosaurs were buried in the sandbox, and now all that remains are the bones. If the participants can unearth some old dinosaur bones, they will be rewarded for their efforts. Give the guests a small prize in exchange for each bone discovered, such as a small dinosaur egg (actually a small foil-covered chocolate egg) or a gold chocolate coin. To make this more challenging for older children, split the kids into a few teams and assign a color to each team. Ask each team to find as many bones in their color as they can.

Dinosaur Egg Relay Race (ages 5 and up) Split the kids into two teams, and give each team one dinosaur egg (actually a hard-boiled egg) and each guest a spoon. Establish a starting line and mark the goal with a chair. The first guest on each team must hold the egg in his spoon, run to the chair, run around it, and run back to line, where he gives the egg to the next person in line. The next player follows the same route while holding the egg in his or her spoon. If the egg is dropped, the runner must start over. The team to finish first wins. After the guests have played this game once, you can introduce another version for them to play, in which the guests must carry the spoons in their mouths.

Dinosaur Story In this wind-down activity, the children are given a noisemaker or a kazoo and sit on the floor in a circle. An adult reads a story about a dinosaur to the group, and every time the main character's name is mentioned, the group toots their kazoos.

Dinosaur Party

Dinosaur Hand Stamps As the guests leave the party, stamp their hands with a dinosaur stamp and ink.

Decorations

Create huge dinosaur footprints on your driveway using sidewalk chalk. Stand a dinosaur atop your mailbox and tie green balloons to the post. Decorate the party room with green streamers and balloons. Place a large dinosaur in the center of the party table and surround it with small plants and moss.

Cake

Make cupcakes and bake an egg into one of them. Frost the cupcakes, sprinkle them with candy confetti, and place a small dinosaur figurine or dinosaur gummy candy on top of each one. Tell the guests that one of the cupcakes contains a dinosaur egg. The guest who receives that cupcake wins a special prize (and another cupcake!) Serve green dinosaur juice (apple juice with food coloring).

Party Favors

Add the suffix "saurus" to each guest's name on the party bags.
Dinosaur figurines
Dinosaur gummy candies
Dinosaur capsules (expand into dinosaur-shaped sponges when immersed in water)
Dinosaur coloring books
Dinosaur stickers
Chocolate (dinosaur) eggs

Teddy Bear Picnic

*For teddy bear lovers, this party is an ideal outdoor celebration—
but can also be transported inside in case of inclement weather.*
Ages: 3 to 5

Invitations

Cut a rectangle of red-and-white checked wrapping paper or fabric. Fold heavyweight invitation paper in half. Glue the red-and-white picnic paper or fabric to the front, and place a teddy bear sticker on the picnic blanket. Under the bear write, "Picnic Time! We're Having a Teddy Bear Picnic to Celebrate Jillian's 3rd Birthday!" Write the party details inside. Ask guests to bring a teddy bear.

Activities

Teddy Bear Dress-Up As guests arrive, they can dress their teddy bears for the picnic. Lay out an assortment of tiny straw hats, scraps of fabric for teddy bear ties or teddy bear togas, ribbons, bows, strings of craft pearls, fake flowers, and old doll clothes for teddy bears of all sizes. Check out your local craft store for accessories.

Old Fashioned Dress-Up Once the teddy bears are dressed up, it's the kids' turn. The guests may place their teddy bears down on a picnic blanket on the ground to watch. Put out old shoes, gloves, hats, ties, shawls, scarves, and costume jewelry. A visit to the thrift shop might be in order! Set up a nail art station and a face painting station as part of the dress-up.

Teddy Bear March Have the kids march around the yard or party room with their teddy bears as you play teddy bear music, such as "Teddy Bear's Picnic" or "Teddy Bear, Teddy Bear."

Teddy Bear Freeze Dance After the march, play some bouncy dance music and have the guests dance with their teddy bears. When the music stops, they must freeze. When the music starts up again, they resume their dancing.

Teddy Bear Awards Present each teddy bear with an award for "Best Dressed," "Prettiest Face," "Biggest Bear," "Fanciest Bear," "Most Colorful Outfit," "Cutest Bear," "Best Bear Personality." Make the mini-awards by cutting award shapes from heavyweight paper, punching a hole in the top, and stringing a ribbon through them. Take instant photos of the children holding their prize-winning teddy bears.

Who Has the Teddy Bear? In the first round, the birthday child is "it" and sits in a chair with her back to the other children while a small teddy bear is placed inside a picnic basket. Meanwhile, the other children sit on the floor in a circle and pass a ball while music is played. When the music stops, the child holding the ball sneaks to the basket, takes the teddy bear, returns to the circle, and hides the teddy bear under his legs or behind his back. The circle of children then chants, "Jillian, Jillian, Who Has the Teddy Bear?" The child who is "it" faces the circle and has three guesses to identify the child who took the teddy bear. The child who took the teddy bear sits in the chair in the next round.

Teddy Bear Stories While the children enjoy their picnic, read them a book about a bear. Give them each a noisemaker or a kazoo and ask them to blow it whenever they hear the title character's name. Then bring on the birthday cupcakes!

Decorations

Two separate picnic blankets are in order, one for the children and one for the teddy bears. Place a miniature tea set on the teddy bear blanket and a child-size tea set on the children's blanket. Serve a light meal from a picnic basket, including sandwiches that have been cut into the shapes of hearts and stars with a cookie cutter.

Cake

Serve two sizes of cupcakes, one for the children and one for their teddy bears. Position graham cracker bears or gummy bears on the tops of the cupcakes.

Party Favors

Teddy bear stickers
Mini teddy bears
Teddy gummy bear candies
Pencils with teddy bear erasers
Teddy bear miniature notebooks
Teddy bear dress-up accessories

Bug Party

*Youngsters who are fascinated with creepy crawly
things will enjoy this buggy celebration.*
Ages: 3 to 6

Invitations

Cut a piece of red colored paper into a circle and glue or draw a black line
down the middle. Add black dots and sticker eyes to resemble a lady bug.
Write, "Buzz on Over to Jacob's for a Buggy Birthday Party!" on the front,
and write the party details on the back.

Activities

Painted Butterflies Get some round coffee filters, watercolor paints,
glitter glue, and black pipe cleaners and lay them out on a table. The kids
paint the coffee filters with a variety of watercolor paints and then apply spots

of glitter glue. An adult helps the children transform the coffee filters into a two-winged butterfly by cinching them with a colored clothespin and attaching a pair of pipe cleaner antennae.

Bug Houses Give each guest a small glass or plastic bug jar, and ask him to create a house for bugs. Guests can decorate the outside of the jars with stickers and colorful rubber bands, and place grass, pebbles, sticks, and acorns inside. Stick a blank label on the top of each jar and let the kids come up with a bug name for an adult to write on the label, along with the name of the bug owner.

Bug Hunt Once the bug houses are decorated, it's time to find some occupants. Before the party, buy a few dozen small plastic bugs and worms and scatter them around a room or the yard. At the party, give the guests plastic spoons and let them pick up as many bugs as they can find and put them into their jars.

Bug Walk Lay several different colors of construction paper in a circle, so there's one square for each guest. Play music while the guests walk around the circle, stepping from one color to the next. When the music stops, every guest should be standing on a piece of construction paper. Pull a color out of a bowl. The children standing on the matching color each win a prize, such as a bug sticker. Use bug names in identifying the colors, such as red ladybug, blue dragonfly, yellow jacket, black fly, orange butterfly, green grasshopper, white moth, and brown caterpillar.

Bug Race Have the kids line up across a starting line, and ask them to race toward a finish line several feet away while they act like bugs. For example, in the first round, ask them to flutter like butterflies toward the finish line. Next, have them crawl like ants, buzz like bees, jump like grasshoppers, buzz like mosquitoes, and squirm like worms. Give all of the guests a small prize after each round—a bug sticker to put on their clothes or a gummy bug to snack on. Hand out homemade awards at the end of the races for the "Best Mosquito," "Best Bumblebee," "Best Worm," "Best Grasshopper," "Best Ant," and so on, making sure that each guest wins an award. Make these paper award ribbons on a home computer or by hand. Punch a hole in each one and string a piece of ribbon through the hole.

Buggy Bodies Stamp the hands of the guests with images of bugs using stamp pads and washable ink, give each guest a temporary bug tattoo, or paint each guest's face with the image of a butterfly, ant, or spider.

Decorations

Use sidewalk chalk to create bug trails leading to the front door: ants, butterflies, bumblebees, and caterpillars. Create some painted butterflies before the party (see the first party activity) and hang these samples around the party room and over the party table. Cover the party table with a plain, white, paper tablecloth and add plenty of bugs—bug stickers, plastic bugs, or bug drawings.

Cake

Bake cupcakes and mix frosting in two different colors. Frost each half of the cupcakes in a different color, and lay a gummy worm across the top of the cupcakes where the two colors meet.

Party Favors

Plastic bugs
Butterfly catchers
Magnifying glasses
Bug jars or cages
Candy bugs and gummy worms
Coloring books with bugs
Bug stickers

Little Engineer Train Party

This party is ideal for the young train enthusiasts and may include a real train ride if you live near a train station.

Ages: 3 to 6

Invitations

Using colored paper and markers, make a jumbo train ticket labeled with phrases such as "The Birthday Express," "Boarding Pass," and "Ashley's Station."

Activities

Train Ride If you live near a train station, plan a train ride on a real train for just one or two stops.

Train Decorating Cut train car shapes out of poster board and lay them out on a table along with train stickers, stamps and inkpads, and markers. As the guests arrive, let each one decorate his own train car. When you're ready for the next activity, sound a train whistle.

Train Store Buy a roll of tickets at a party goods store, and hide a few dozen around the party room or yard. Have kids hunt for the tickets and pick up all that they find. Then invite kids to the Train Store, where they can buy snacks and party favors with the tickets they found, such as bags of popcorn, candy, pretzels, red bandannas, and engineer hats.

Train Ticket Relay Race (ages 5 and up) Split the kids into two teams and give each team an index card, which is their train ticket. Establish a starting line and a finish line marked by a chair that's set up with two hole punchers or an ink pad with two stamps. The first guest in each line must run to the Train Station (the chair), stamp or punch his team train ticket, bring it back to line, and hand it to the next child in line. The next child runs to the train station, stamps or punches the ticket, and brings it back to the next guest in line. The first team to have all its members stamp or punch the team ticket wins.

Train Tracks (ages 4 and up) Establish a starting line and a finish line several yards away from each other. The guests are each assigned a train car color by drawing slips of colored paper out of a bowl. Players must stand behind the starting line to be safe. An adult stands between the starting line and the finish line and calls out train car colors one by one, such as, "Red train cars," "Blue train cars," and so on. As each color is called out, the kids assigned that color must race to the finish line and cross it without being tagged by the adult. Any kids who are tagged become helpers and try to tag other kids as they run by. When the adult yells, "Train Tracks!" then all remaining players behind the start line must race to the finish line. Continue playing several rounds.

Freeze Train Play some train music, such as "I've Been Working on the Railroad," "She'll Be Coming 'Round the Mountain When She Comes," or "Train Keeps a Rolling." Ask the kids to make train movements as the music plays. When the music stops, everyone must freeze.

Train Toot (ages 3 to 4) Give the guests each a small plastic whistle and ask them to sit on the floor in a circle. Read a short book about trains and ask the kids to toot their whistles every time they hear a certain word or the main character's name.

Decorations

Decorate the party room with toy trains and poster board Railroad Crossing signs. Select primary colors for balloons, streamers, and paper goods.

Cake

Start with two cake mixes and make four small, rectangular cakes using loaf pans. Line up the four cars behind one another, leaving a small space between each car. Frost each train car with a different color of frosting and then sprinkle a different kind of candy on each car, such as mini M&Ms, sprinkles, jelly beans, chocolate chips, and red licorice drops. Use round candy wafers for wheels on the sides of each train car.

Party Favors

Train stickers

Train schedules
Tickets
Train cars
Whistles
Red bandannas
Books about trains
Train coloring books

Chocolate Factory Party

*This party is the perfect choice for the birthday child
who loves candy and the fantasy of a chocolate factory.*
Ages: 3 to 6

Invitations

Use candy wrappers as the invitation envelope. An M&Ms wrapper works fine. Create small invitations decorated with candy stickers. Fold and insert one inside each candy wrapper. Place the wrapper inside a regular envelope for mailing. The invitation can read, "Yummy! You're invited to Lauren's Candy Factory to celebrate her third birthday. Come find a golden ticket and take a tour of the enchanted candy factory."

Activities

Candy Party Hat Set out strips of candy dots, glue sticks, and solid-colored birthday party hats. Let each kid decorate a hat with candy.

Money Hunt Buy one toy wallet for each guest as a party favor. Place some play money inside the wallets and hide each wallet in a different spot within a designated area. Explain that the guests must find some money so they can buy candy at the candy store. Direct the guests to the designated area and have them search until each child has found a wallet.

Candy Store Once all the guest have wallets with money, they can buy candy bars at the candy store and then open them to see if theirs contain a golden ticket that will entitle them to a tour of the candy factory. Before the party, buy a miniature candy bar for each guest, insert a "golden ticket" inside each wrapper (use a slip of gold-colored paper), and re-wrap the candy bars. An older sibling or another parent can play the role of the Candy Man and sell the candy to the children. Give the children plenty of time to open their candy bars and find their golden tickets.

Candy Tunnel To get to the Candy Factory, the children must crawl through the Candy Tunnel. Use an old appliance box as the tunnel. Drape colorful sheets over it and decorate it with streamers and candies. Once the guests crawl out the other end, give them each a goodie bag to use to collect candy throughout the factory.

Factory Tour Designate a room or an area of your yard as the candy factory. Set up a few stations where kids can play a game and win candy. Ask other parents to help out by manning the candy stations.

Balloon Tree Insert small candies (candy straws and rolls of Smarties) into deflated balloons and then blow them up. Using ribbon, tie each balloon to a branch of a real or artificial tree. Let each guest select a balloon. The parent pops the balloon and then gives the guest the candy inside.

Penny Candy Gather several one-gallon plastic milk or water jugs and cut a large opening in each one. Fill them with different kinds of candies, such as M&Ms, Tootsie Rolls, Hershey's Kisses, Raisinets, and so on. Place a scoop or a large spoon in each jug, and let the guests buy a few scoops of candy with the money in their wallets.

Candy Cups Hide a variety of miniature candy bars under several inverted cups. Let guests select a cup and win the candy they find underneath it.

Coin Toss Give each guest five pennies to toss into bowls and pie plates. Reward their efforts with a piece of candy.

Candy Dig Place several pieces of individually wrapped candy in the bottom of a large basket. Cover the candy with popcorn. Let each guest dig to find a piece of candy.

Lollipop Tree Stick large lollipops into a pot and attach a sticker to each one. Put matching stickers in a bowl. Let the guests each draw a sticker out of the bowl and then find the lollipop with the matching sticker.

Decorations

The candy factory should be colorful and festive, decorated with balloons, streamers, real lollipops dangling from ribbons, and Christmas lights. Create a candy throne for the birthday child by taping candy bar wrappers all over a chair.

Cake

Create a Candy Cake by decorating a frosted sheet cake with several different types of candy and lollipops. The birthday child will enjoy helping! Serve juice with licorice straws, which are sticks of licorice with the ends cut off.

Party Favors

Wallets
Play money
Candy
Candy stickers

Banana Split Party

*A highly original party that's loads of fun for kids
with a broad range of ages and interests.*
Ages: 3 to 7

Invitations

Cut yellow paper into the shape of a banana and decorate it with stickers of ice cream cones, floats, and sundaes. Write the party details length-wise on the banana.

Activities

Banana Socks Give each guest a pair of yellow socks or a cap and set out fabric paints, fabric pens, puff fabric paints, and fabric glitter paints. Let the kids decorate the socks or caps with bananas, stars, hearts and other shapes.

Banana Hunt Hide several dozen yellow candies throughout an area of the house or yard. Give the guests party bags and let them race to pick up as many banana candies as they can.

Hot Banana Before the party, write numbers on several real bananas using a permanent marker. You should have one banana for each guest. At the party, have the kids sit on the floor in a circle. Give a banana to each guest, and ask them to pass the bananas from guest to guest while music plays. When the music stops, draw a number out of a bowl. The guest holding the banana with the matching number wins a small prize. Continue playing until everyone has won a prize. If there are more than six or eight guests at the party, then draw two or three numbers from the bowl during each round.

Banana Race Have the guests line up and place bananas on top of their heads. The children race to the finish line while balancing the bananas on their heads, then all the racers are rewarded with party favors. At parties for older children, this game can be a banana relay race.

Banana Piñata Make a Piñata out of a yellow gift bag. Cut out the bottom and loosely tape it back in place. Then fill the bag with candy, small toys, and yellow confetti. Hang it from the ceiling or a tree by a string run through the handles. Decorate it with yellow streamers, yellow balloons and hanging yellow banana shapes cut from poster board.

Ice Cream Making Help each guest place a half of a cup of whole milk, 1 tablespoon of sugar, and one-half teaspoon of vanilla in a sandwich-size resealable bag. Guests seal this bag and place it inside a gallon-size resealable bag that's filled with ice cubes and salt. Guests shake the bags for about ten minutes until the mixture is transformed into soft ice cream. (Play music to keep things interesting!) The homemade ice cream is then used to make banana splits in the next activity.

Banana Splits Set out all the ingredients for banana splits, including maraschino cherries, chocolate sprinkles, hot fudge, strawberries, M&Ms, crushed Oreo's, sliced bananas, ice cream, and whipped cream, and have the kids assemble their own banana splits.

Banana Split Party

Decorations

Hang real bananas (or banana shapes cut from yellow poster board) from the ceiling and around the party room using ribbon or streamers. Dangle yellow ribbons over the entrance to the party room. Draw bananas on the driveway and walkway using yellow sidewalk chalk. Decorate the bushes with yellow streamers and yellow balloons, and put out a banana-shaped "Banana Split Party This Way" sign in the front yard. Decorate a throne in yellow streamers and yellow balloons for the birthday child. Use solid yellow party hats, tablecloths, plates, cups, and so on.

Cake

Add yellow food coloring to the white cake mix just before pouring it into a sheet cake pan. Once it's baked and cooled, cut the cake into the shape of a giant banana. Frost it yellow and outline it with black icing. Serve the cake after the guests have made their banana splits.

Party Favors

Mini ice cream scoops
Stickers of ice cream cones or bananas
Small memo pads (ice cream cone shape or banana shape)
Banana pens
Decorated banana socks
Banana candy
Real bananas
Yellow nail polish
Banana flavored lip-gloss
Yellow crazy straws

Little Mermaid Party

*For the child who is intrigued by the story of the little mermaid
and the sea, this party is a real-life fantasy.*
Ages: 3 to 7

Invitations

Cut colored paper into the shape of a starfish or an octopus with wavy legs. Write the invitation information in the center of the starfish. Outline it with glue and sprinkle with glitter.

Activities

Sea Treasures Lay out seashells—actually uncooked pasta shells in jumbo, medium, and small sizes that have been spray painted before the party—and give each guest a treasure chest made from a kids' size shoebox that has been spray painted gold. Lay out glitter glue, glue sticks, fake jewels, and stickers for the arriving guests to use to decorate the treasure chests. The seashells can be decorated with markers and glitter glue and then placed inside the treasure chests. The small seashells may be glued to the top of the treasure chest.

Fin Race Give guests the chance to see what it's like to walk on fins with this game. Give each guest a pillowcase. Line them up at the starting line and ask them to step into their pillowcases and hop to the finish line. At parties for older children, you may want to add stunts (like a turnaround) or obstacles (like a chair to circle) to the race. You may want to give the guests a practice run and award special prizes to the first, second, and third place mermaids. Give all the kids a prize to place in their treasure chests for finishing the race.

Crab Race To walk like a crab, guests walk on their hands and feet, but in a belly-up position with their backs facing down. At parties for 3-, 4-, and 5-year-olds, the children race from a start line to a finish line, where small party favors are handed out to all finishers. For 6-year-olds and older, have a Crab Relay Race. Split the guests into two teams. Establish a goal line with two chairs and have one child from each team walk like a crab to the chairs, circle the chairs, and return to line. Then the next child in line walks like a crab to the chair, circles it, and returns to the line. Continue playing until one team has finished. Award party favor prizes to be stashed in the treasure chests.

Mermaid Circle Ahead of time, tape several pieces of construction paper (in a few different colors) to the floor in a circular pattern, each a couple of steps away from the next. Place a mermaid figurine on the floor in the center of the circle. Create corresponding slips of colored paper and put them in a bowl or hat. At the party, play music as the children march around the circle, stepping from color to color. When the music stops, each child should be standing on a color. An adult draws a color out of the bowl, and the children who are standing on that color each win a small prize or lollipop. Play several times, until all the guests have won at least one prize.

Mermaid, Mermaid, Who Has the Shell? In the first round of this game, the birthday child is the Mermaid and is sent to sit in a chair with her back to the other children, wearing a crown, while a shell is placed on the floor behind the Mermaid's chair. Meanwhile, the other children sit on the floor in a circle and pass a ball while music is played. When the music stops, the child holding the ball sneaks to the chair, takes the Mermaid's shell, returns to the circle, and hides the shell under his legs. The circle of children then chants, "Mermaid, Mermaid, Who Has the Shell?" The Mermaid faces the circle and has three guesses to identify the child who took her shell. The child who took the shell becomes the Mermaid or Merman in the next round.

Ocean Floor This game determines which team each guest will belong to in the following Treasure Hunt activity. Each team should have about three or four children, and the teams can be named after underwater creatures, such as starfish, sharks, eels, crabs, octopuses, fish, and dolphins. Before the party, get a small, resealable plastic bag for each child, and place one sticker of a sea creature into each plastic bag, corresponding with the team name. Drop the bags into a children's wading pool (bathtub or a large pot if the party's indoors) that's filled with water. At the party, add bubble bath and more water to the pool and give each guest the chance to reach in and grab a bag to determine which team he will be on. Children may wear the stickers as a reminder of which team they're on for the next activity. Toss a few dozen coins on the ocean floor, too, for the children to pick up and place in their treasure chests.

Treasure Hunt Create a simple treasure hunt where kids search for the hidden sea creature assigned to their team. (Teams are designated based on the Ocean Floor activity above.) The creatures can be small, plastic sea animals, stickers, shapes cut out of construction paper, or candy sea creatures.

Make sure you hide several sea creatures for each team to find. At the end of the game, teams keep their sea creatures or trade them in for a prize, such as a chocolate gold coin for each sea creature found. Guests store their prizes in the treasure chests they decorated earlier.

Under the Sea Weather permitting, ask guests to wear a bathing suit to the party. Set up a vacillating sprinkler. As the water spray rotates, the guests must race under the spray arch from one side of the sprinkler to the other without getting wet. Hand out prizes once they've made five trips under the sea.

Mermaid Treasure Balls Before the party, make one or two Mermaid Treasure Balls by wrapping party favors or candy in crepe paper streamers. Start by winding the crepe paper around the first piece of candy. Add another piece of candy and continue to wind the crepe paper around it, and another, and so on, until you have several pieces of candy wrapped in a crepe paper ball, about the size of a softball. You should have twice as many favors as party guests, to be sure that each guest will receive at least one. At the party, the guests sit on the floor in a circle and pass the treasure ball as you play music. When the music stops, the guest holding the treasure ball unwinds the crepe paper to find a treasure. Continue playing until the last treasure has been unwrapped. If there are eight or more kids at the party, pass two treasure balls around the circle simultaneously.

Decorations

Decorate the party room or yard to look like an ocean, with blue and green streamers and balloons. Hang streamers and ribbons in the doorway of the party room. Hang a colorful fish net and stick plastic starfish, shells, fish and seahorses onto the net and in other spots around the room. Cover the party table with blue cellophane. Place an open treasure chest or jewelry box in the center of the table, and place an overflowing bounty of sea treasures in the box, such as beads, gold chocolate coins, seashells, coral, starfish, and fake jewels. Sprinkle some sand (you can use light brown sugar) around the treasure chest. Decorate several jumbo pasta shells with spray paint, glitter, and sequins and put one at each place setting.

Cake

Mermaid cakes may be available at your local bakery, grocery store, or ice cream parlor. You can make your own by decorating a sheet cake with a mermaid scene. Start with a blue frosting background, and then add colorful icing waves, a brown sugar "island" mound, and toy figurines of a mermaid, a crab, a fish, and an octopus. Serve the cake with clear cups of lukewarm sparkling water or clear soda, and give the kids blue and green ice cubes (made from water and food coloring) to drop into the water. Throughout the party, serve bowls of goldfish- or dolphin-shaped crackers for the children to munch on.

Party Favors

Costume jewelry
Gold chocolate coins
Fish squirt toys
Beach toys
Mermaid coloring books
Plastic sea horses and fish
Red licorice fish
Ocean creature capsules (expand when immersed in water)
Bubbles
Fish net bags
Treasure chests
Decorated shells

Young Pajama Party

Surprise! This is not a sleepover party! If your child is too young for a sleepover party but wants one anyway, here's a great compromise. Enjoy the thrill of a nighttime pajama party but send your guests home before bedtime.

Ages: 3 to 8

Invitations

This party can begin after dinner and end a couple of hours later. For the invitation, start with a photo (or a drawing) of the birthday child in pajamas. Glue this to a piece of paper and add large, open stars in the sky above. Inside each star, write a piece of party information. For example, "Sarah's Pajama Party!" in the first star, the date and time in the second star, the address in the next star, "Come dressed in your PJ's!" in the next star, "Super Snacks," "Silly Games," "Bring Your Sleeping Bag," in other stars, and so on. Go to a copy center to have the drawing copied onto brightly colored paper.

Activities

Get Ready For Bed Let the kids play with facial cleanser, moisturizer, temporary tattoos, curlers, brushes, combs, ribbons, hair clips, dental floss, lip gloss, and so on, as they prepare for bed.

Nail Art Enlist the help of a teenager to paint designs on the guests' fingernails using nail polish. Designs may include stripes, flowers, dots, lightning bolts, and cow patches.

Hair Beading Braid a small strand of each guest's hair, put beads over the braid, and wrap an elastic band several times around the bottom to prevent the beads from falling off.

Freeze Brush Before the party, use puff paint to write each guest's name on a toothbrush. Hand out the toothbrushes at the party and play some lively music while the children vigorously brush their teeth. When the music stops, everyone must freeze in place. Provide a few different flavors and brands of toothpaste to make it interesting.

Bouncing Contest Place a double bed mattress (or two) on the floor and let the children bounce on the beds while you blast familiar tunes. Encourage the guests to sing and bounce to the music. Hand out awards for "High Jumper," "Silly Jumper," "Peppy Jumper," "Loud Jumper," "Fast Jumper," "Long Jumper," "Happy Jumper," and so on. Take instant photos or videotape this activity to watch later.

Flashlight Tag All the guests hide in the party room while the birthday child counts to ten. The birthday child then uses a flashlight to find the hiding guests. The first child to be struck by a beam of light from the flashlight is "it" in the next round. Continue playing for several rounds.

Pillow Relay Race (ages 5 and up) Split the guests into two teams and establish a starting line and a goal line. Give each team a small pillow. One at a time, each guest must place the pillow on top of his head and run to the goal line and back without dropping it. The winning team goes first in the next game.

Huckle Buckle Beanstalk Use a toy spider or other object slightly smaller than a child's fist. The birthday child hides this in the party room while all the guests are in another room. It must be hidden in a location that is visible without moving anything in the room. Once the spider is hidden, the birthday child calls the guests back into the party room. The first guest to spot the hidden spider yells, "Huckle Buckle Beanstalk!" and then it's that guest's turn to hide it on the next round. Continue playing for several rounds.

Root Beer Floats When it's time for a midnight snack, the guests can make their own root beer floats and Coke floats. An adult scoops ice cream into a tall glass, then the guests can pour root beer or Coke over the ice cream. Hand out straws and spoons.

Sleeping Bag Fun Lay out blankets, sleeping bags, comforters, and pillows on the floor and let the kids pretend it's bedtime. Put a few fake bugs under the blankets for some fun. Turn the lights down, play some recorded lullabies, and have a contest to see how long the children can be silent. Set an alarm clock to go off after a few minutes.

Spin the Bottle When it's time for the birthday child to open her presents, have the guests sit on the floor in a circle with their presents on their laps. Put a bottle in the center of the circle, and have the birthday child spin it to determine whose gift she'll open next.

Decorations

Hang an old pair of pajamas on your front door. Drape pajamas over your bushes, your lamppost, and so on. Hang a clothesline in the party room and pin pajamas to it. Decorate the party room ceiling with glow-in-the-dark stars and planets and holiday lights. Hang poster board stars and moons in the doorway to the party room, along with ribbon and streamers. Put colored light bulbs in your lamps. Throw a pile of pillows and stuffed animals in the corner of the room.

Cake

Make a two-layer rectangular sheet cake. To make the cake look like a sleeping bag, cut a few inches off the end of the top layer before applying the frosting. Once the cake is frosted, lay a doll head on the bottom tier, as if the doll's body is inside the sleeping bag cake. Decorate the sides of the sleeping bag with a zigzag line of blue or gray frosting resembling a zipper.

Party Favors

Personalized toothbrushes
Glow-in-the-dark stickers
Glow-in-the-dark balls
Glow-in-the-dark bracelets
Mini flashlights
Hair clips
Nail polish

Pirate Island Party

Partygoers will find this world of pirates and buried treasures intriguing and fun!
Ages: 3 to 8

Invitations

Create a pirate's map to your house and use stickers or computer clip-art to add images of treasure chests, skulls and crossbones, a ship, gold coins, a parrot, and a pirate's hat. Write, "Ahoy mates! Brave the high seas and come join Captain Sam and his friends on Pirate Island to celebrate his 5th birthday!" Photocopy the master onto ivory or brown paper. If the invitations will be hand-delivered, roll them up scroll-style, tie a ribbon around them, insert them into a small bottle, and deliver the bottles.

Activities

Eye Patches Before the party, cut craft foam into eye patches and punch two holes in the top of each eye patch. At the party, set out the patches along with string or shoelaces and gel pens, paint pens, or paints. The kids decorate eye patches with the pens and then thread the string through the holes. Although black eye patches are more authentic, the kids may also enjoy brightly colored patches.

Pirate Dress-Up The kids dress up as pirates with eye patches, bandannas, temporary tattoos, fabric sashes, and gold curtain rings as hoop earrings. Give them face paint and help them draw on stubble and beards. Take an instant photo of each for the party favor bag.

Walk the Plank Before the party, get a long, wooden board (at least 8 feet (8') long) and section off squares with a marker, so there's a square for each guest. Write a number in each square. (If you don't have a piece of wood, draw it on your driveway using sidewalk chalk or write numbers in paper plates and tape them to the floor in a straight line.) At the party, explain to the kids that they are pirates and the plank represents safety, but it can hold only one pirate per square, and that the area of the floor outside the plank is shark-infested water. The pirates walk down the length of the plank, stepping from one square to the next. When they reach the end of the plank, they rush back to the beginning and start walking down it again, one step at a time. Music is played while the pirates are walking down the plank. When the music stops, each pirate will be standing on a number. Draw a number out of a bowl, and the pirate standing on the corresponding number wins a gold chocolate coin. Play several rounds, and award a special prize to the pirate with the most chocolate coins at the end. If you expect more than six guests at your party, you can draw two or three numbers out of the bowl in each round to keep this game moving quickly.

Sword Hunt Before the party, hide a few dozen miniature plastic cocktail swords around the yard or party room. Get a velvety drawstring loot bag (an old drawstring pocketbook would work) and fill it with play coins, chocolate gold coins, and candy. At the party, the kids hunt for the plastic swords. When they find one, they can trade it in for a prize in the pirate loot bag, and then they can resume their hunt. At parties for older children, you can divide the kids into teams and assign point values based on the color of the swords.

Treasure Hunt (ages 6 and up). Before the party, create a treasure chest by covering a box with aluminum foil and strapping belts around it. Fill the box with chocolate gold coins, pennies, costume jewelry, candy, fake coins, fake dollar bills, uncooked jumbo pasta shells, and treasure balls (refer to the Party Favors for a description). Bury or hide the treasure chest. Create a treasure map that leads to the hidden treasure chest. Cut the map into several pieces, so there's one piece for each guest. Roll each piece up scroll-style, tie it with a ribbon, and slip each piece into a separate bottle. Float the bottles in a children's wading pool or a bathtub. At the party, each guest selects a bottle and removes his piece of the map. The guests assemble the overall map together by gluing the pieces onto a large piece of construction paper using glue sticks. Once the map is pieced together, the children use it to find the hidden treasure chest. The kids can each take a treasure ball and a handful of trinkets from the chest. At parties with more than eight guests, you may consider creating two copies of the treasure map and having two teams race to assemble the map and find the location of the hidden treasure.

Pirate Islands Lay four blankets or large towels in the yard about 10' or 15' away from each other. Each blanket should be a different color and will represent a different pirate island. To begin, the birthday child sits in the center of the blankets, wears a blindfold or closes his eyes, and counts to ten while the party guests run to any of the four "islands." Without looking, the birthday child calls out a color. All of the pirates on the island of that color are captured and must go to the center and help the birthday child count in the next round. Together, they count to ten while the remaining guests race to a new blanket. Again, the birthday child calls out a color without looking at the blankets, and all the pirates on that island are captured and must move to the center. Play continues until there is only one pirate left sailing the seas. That pirate becomes the counter in the next game, and all the other guests return to the sea.

Pass the Pirate's Parcel (ages 4 and up) Before the party, find a series of boxes that nest inside each other. In the smallest box, place a small party favor for each guest. Wrap this box and then place the wrapped present in the next biggest box. Wrap this, and keep going until the largest box is wrapped. At the party, play music as the kids pass the present from one child to the next. When the music stops, the child holding the box opens it. If it's another wrapped box, start the music, and the box gets passed again. Keep going until the final box is opened. Each child gets a favor from the smallest box.

Decorations

Decorate with model ships, black streamers, and black party hats. Draw a treasure map on a large sheet of paper and use it for the tablecloth. Put out cups of crayons and markers so the kids can add to the map. Use black paper plates, cups, and napkins.

Cake

Decorate a sheet cake with a pirate scene. Start with blue or green frosting for the ocean and add a sandy island using brown sugar. Then add small figurines to the cake, such as a ship, a pirate, a gold treasure chest on the island, skull and crossbones, and so on. Add small candies such as silver balls lying around the treasure chest. Bake a raw bean into the cake and give a special prize to the guest who gets the treasure bean in his piece of cake.

Party Favors

Make a miniature treasure box for each child by covering shoeboxes with aluminum foil and attaching a sticker label with their names. The kids can use these to collect their treasures throughout the party.

Miniature kaleidoscopes
Eye patches
Toy ships
Gold chocolate coins
Treasure balls

(Make treasure balls by wrapping party favors or candy in crepe paper. Start by winding the crepe paper around the first favor several times. Add another favor and continue to wind the crepe paper, and another, and so on, until you have a few favors and candies wrapped in a crepe paper ball, which should be about the size of a softball. Cover the balls with tin foil. Create a treasure ball for each guest.)

Purple Party

If your child is wild about the color purple, this unique party is sure to please!
Ages: 3 to 8

Invitations

Cut heavy purple paper into rectangles and fold each one in half. On the outside cover, draw a design (a lightning bolt, cloud, sunburst, mountain, star, or flower) in glue, and then sprinkle purple and silver glitter on the glue. Write "Emily's Purple Party!" on the cover of the invitation. Inside, list the party details and ask guests to wear an article of purple clothing.

Activities

Party Hat Decorating Buy solid purple party hats and set them out on a table with glue, glitter, stickers, and small purple objects (like purple plastic worms, purple stickers, purple feathers, purple beads, or purple buttons). As kids arrive, let them decorate their own party hats.

Purple Party

Purple People Help the kids become "Purple People" by applying purple face paint, purple lipstick, purple eye shadow, and purple nail polish. Take a group photo!

Pass the Purple Present Before the party, find a series of boxes that nest inside each other. In the smallest box, place a small, purple party favor for each guest, such as grape lip-gloss, purple figurines, or purple pens. Wrap this box, and then put this wrapped present in the next size box. Wrap this box, and keep going until the largest box is wrapped, and you have a series of nested presents. At the party, have the kids sit on the floor in a circle. Play music as the kids pass the present from one child to the next. When the music stops, the kid holding the box unwraps it. If it's another wrapped box, start the music, and the box gets passed again. Keep going until the final box is unwrapped, and then each child gets a purple present from the smallest box.

Purple Hunt Cut purple-colored paper into several different shapes— stars, hearts, circles, squares, ovals, triangles, rectangles, and diamonds. Make sure there's a unique shape for each guest. Cut at least four copies of each shape. Place one copy of each shape in a bowl and hide the others. At the party, let the kids each draw one shape out of the bowl, and send them off to find two more of that shape in a particular area of the house or yard. Once they have collected three of the same shape, they can return for their prize: a piece of purple candy or a party favor. For 3-year-olds, you may conduct a Purple Candy Hunt or a Purple Peanut Hunt instead, where you hide a few dozen individually wrapped purple candies or purple spray-painted peanuts in an area of the house or yard and give each guest a purple bag to pick up as many candies as they can.

Purple Mummy Split the kids into two teams and give each team a roll of purple crepe paper and a few purple bows. At "Go!" the teams each select one guest who agrees to be wrapped, and the team proceeds to wrap that guest's body in the purple crepe paper, mummy-style. NOTE: no wrapping on the neck or face! Once the guest is wrapped, the purple bows are added. The first team to finish wrapping their mummy wins.

Purple Piñata Make a Piñata out of a purple gift bag, cutting out the bottom and loosely taping it back in place. Fill it with candy, small toys, and purple confetti. Run a string through the handles and hang it from the ceiling. Decorate it with streamers and balloons in different shades of purple.

Decorations

Decorate the front of your home and the party room in purple, using purple balloons, purple streamers, purple tablecloths, and purple ribbons hanging from the top of the doorway to the party room. Draw designs on the sidewalk and driveway using purple sidewalk chalk. Decorate a purple throne for the birthday child. Use purple light bulbs in lamps in the party room to cast a purple glow.

Cake

Make a white cake. While the cake is baking, make a mix of grape gelatin and set it out to cool, but don't refrigerate it yet. About 15 minutes after removing the cake from the oven poke a few dozen holes in the top of it using a birthday candle. Pour the liquid grape gelatin on top of the cake, letting it fill the holes in the top of the cake. Once it's cool, frost the cake with purple frosting and decorate it with purple candies and sprinkles. When the cake is cut, it will have streaks of purple inside. Write "Happy Purple Birthday, Sarah!" on the cake. Serve with room temperature 7-Up or Sprite and purple ice cubes (made by mixing purple food coloring with water), which will turn the soda purple as they melt.

Party Favors

Place the party favors inside a jumbo, plastic purple cup, a purple bag, or a purple sand pail.

Purple nylon wallets
Purple pocket mirrors
Purple socks
Purple pens or pencils
Purple nail polish
Purple lip gloss
Purple bubble bath
Purple hairbrushes, hair combs, or hair clips
Purple cars or trucks
Instant photos of Purple People

Valentine Tea Party

A sweet tea party with a heart theme, this celebration includes dressing up.
Ages: 3 to 8

Invitations

Cut a piece of heavyweight colored paper into a heart shape and punch holes around the border. Weave a long piece of ribbon in and out of the holes, creating a border around the edge of the card. Write the party details in the center. Ask the guests to dress up for a Valentine tea party! Decorate the outside of the envelope with heart and teacup stickers.

Activities

Potpourri Sachets Lay out ribbon, dried potpourri, and a variety of heart-patterned fabrics cut into 6" x 6" squares. The guests each select a fabric square, place some potpourri in the center of it, twist it, and tie a ribbon around it. Older guests may be able to stitch heart-shaped sachets closed, or iron fusing or fabric glue may be used. At parties for younger children, the kids can glue potpourri and heart stickers to solid pink or red birthday party hats using a glue stick.

Valentine Gingerbread House Ahead of time, gather and clean a one-pint milk carton for each child. Break up some graham crackers so they're the same size as the sides of the milk cartons. Fill cupcake tins with several different kinds of Valentine candy decorations, and put a few different colors of frosting in individual bowls or plates. Older children may be able to handle pastry bags. At the party, the children create Valentine Gingerbread Houses by attaching the graham crackers to the milk carton, and then decorating the gingerbread with rows and dots of Valentine candy, using frosting as the glue. Make one house before the party as a sample.

Valentine Dress-Up Provide dress-up clothes, jewelry, shoes, purses, and hats for the children to try on. Set up a manicure station, a temporary tattoo station, and a face painting station where an adult paints a heart on the face of each guest. Once they're all dressed, take a photo.

Valentine Treasure Hunt Buy two or three kinds of inexpensive children's Valentines and scatter these in hiding places throughout the party room or yard. At the party, split the guests into two or three teams by having them draw a Valentine out of a bowl. The teams work together to pick up as many matching Valentines as they can find. Once they're finished, the teams each count the number of Valentines that they found. Hand out party favors to everyone, but give each team a different favor or a different color favor.

Teacup Relay Race (ages 6 and up) Split the guests into two teams. Give each team a teacup half-filled with water and a saucer. The first member of each team, the captain, must pass the teacup and saucer to the next player, who passes to the next player, and so on until the teacup reaches the end of the line. At that point, the last person in line must run to the front of the line, and then the team passes the teacup down the line again. When it reaches the last person in line, that player runs to the front, and the team passes the teacup down the line again. The relay race continues until one team's captain is at the front of the line again. If the water is spilled, the team must start over.

Valentine Piñata Make a Valentine Piñata out of a pink or red gift bag. Cut out the bottom and tape it loosely back into place. Fill the bag with valentine candy, small toys, and red, white, and pink confetti. Decorate it with red and pink ribbons and streamers and heart cutouts. Run a string through the handles to hang it from the ceiling.

Tea Time Invite the guests into the tea salon, where you serve them warm (not hot), flavored, decaffeinated tea in little teacups, strawberry milk, and sugar.

Decorations

Decorate the tea salon with flowers, unlit candles, a lacey tablecloth and napkins, a tea set, and pretend-china. Use a doily at each guest's place setting. Scatter candy hearts on the table. Decorate the birthday child's throne with hearts and red, white, and pink streamers. Hang poster board hearts and heart-shaped balloons around the party room with ribbon.

Cake

Bake heart-shaped cupcakes using round cupcake tins! To do this, insert a marble between the side of each individual cupcake tin and the paper liner. Once each cupcake is baked and the marble is removed, there will be an indentation in the top of the cupcakes to make it heart-shaped. Frost the cupcakes with pink frosting, and outline the heart shape with red icing. Sprinkle a few Valentine candies on each cupcake. If you will be serving a meal, use a cookie cutter to make heart-shaped pizzas, heart-shaped sandwiches, or heart-shaped pancakes.

Party Favors

Valentine stickers
Valentine gingerbread houses
Valentine candy
Pencils with hearts
Notepads with heart motif
Valentine coloring books

Parties for Children Ages 4 -10

Firefighter Party

*This party may include a tour of your local fire department
for a touch of realism and education.*
Ages: 4 to 7

Invitations

Fold rectangles of colored paper in half and decorate the cover with stickers
of dalmatians, fire trucks, and flames. Write, "It's Joshua's Four-Alarm
Firefighter Party!" on the cover and list the party details inside.

Activities

Fire Station Tour Call your local fire department to see if they'll give the
kids an educational tour and let them climb into a fire truck. Many provide
this service for free or for a small donation.

Firefighter Party Bags Get white paper bags for the guests and stencil
each guest's name onto a bag. Lay the bags out on a table along with
firefighter stickers, markers, and crayons, and let the guests decorate their
party bags as they arrive.

Firefighter Party

Huckle Buckle Beanstalk Get a small toy fire truck (no larger than a child's fist) and show it to all the kids. The birthday child then hides the truck somewhere in a room while the guests wait in another room. The hidden truck must be visible without moving anything in the room. The waiting kids are called in once the truck is hidden, and with their hands behind their backs, they walk around the room looking for the hidden truck. As soon as a guest spots it, he yells "Huckle Buckle Beanstalk!" Then that guest hides the truck while the others wait in another room, and another round of the game is played.

Firefighter Relay Race (ages 5 and up) Split the kids into two teams, and establish a start line and a goal marked by a chair for each team. Place a firefighter's hat and a rain slicker on the chair. The first child in each team must run to the chair, put on the hat and slicker, run back to line, and pass the hat and slicker to the next child in line. That child wears the hat and slicker while he runs to the chair, runs around the chair, and returns to line to hand the hat and slicker to the next child, and so on. The last child in line leaves the hat and slicker on the chair. The first team to leave the firefighter's hat on the chair wins. Award both teams with small party favors to put in their bags.

Hot Potato Before the party, gather several potatoes, one for each guest, and mark each potato with a number using a permanent marker. The kids sit on the floor in a circle and each holds a potato. When the music begins, the kids pass the potatoes quickly around the circle. When the music stops, each child should be holding one potato. Draw a number out of a firefighter hat. The guest holding the potato with the number drawn wins a prize. Continue playing until all the guests have won a prize. If the party has more than six or eight guests, then draw two or more numbers on each round to keep the game moving quickly.

Paper Match Wrap a party favor for each guest, using a different wrapping paper for each one. Tie a red helium balloon to each gift, and scatter the bags throughout the yard or party room. Have the kids each draw a square of wrapping paper out of a fire hat and then find the party favor with the matching paper.

Firefighter Piñata Cut the bottom out of a red shopping bag or gift bag and then loosely tape it back in place. Place candy, play money, party favors, and red tissue paper confetti inside the gift bag. Decorate the bag with red and silver ribbon, streamers, and balloons. Run string through the handles and hang it in the party room.

Decorations

Use firefighter hats instead of birthday hats, and write each guest's name on the front of a hat using a permanent marker. Decorate the party table with fire trucks, dalmatians, and fire hydrants. Use a red and silver color scheme for crepe paper, balloons, paper plates, tablecloth, and napkins. Decorate the outside of the house with red and silver balloons.

Cake

Bake a layer cake, frost it with a base of white frosting, and then embellish it with streaks of yellow, red, and orange frosting on the sides. Perch a small fire truck on top.

Party Favors

Miniature fire trucks
Dalmatian spotted pencils
Squirt toys
Firefighter hats
Dalmatian figurines or stuffed animals
Coloring books

Mexican Fiesta

Tacos, piñatas, and confetti are the elements of fun in this fiesta!
Ages: 4 to 7

Invitations

Fold a rectangle of colored paper in half and decorate the cover with small bits of yellow, orange, and red tissue paper squares. Use a paintbrush and a mixture of half glue and half water to attach the squares. Use markers to add spiraling squiggles to represent falling streamers. Write "Hannah's Fiesta!" across the cover of the invitation, and write the party details inside.

Activities

Confetti Sprinkle Have the kids throw colorful confetti on guests as they arrive. Buy pre-made confetti or make it by cutting red, yellow, and orange tissue paper into small squares. If the party's held outside, substitute grass seed or birdseed for confetti.

Uno, Dos, Tres Establish two lines that are at least twenty or thirty yards apart. You may use sidewalk chalk on a driveway to draw the lines, or identify markers as boundaries. Kids line up behind one line, while an adult stands behind the other line. The adult yells a number between one and ten in Spanish, such as "Tres!", and the kids all take that number of steps towards the adult. The adult continues calling numbers and the kids keep stepping towards the adult's line. When the adult yells "Cumpleanos!" (the Spanish word for birthday), the guests must run back to their line for safety while the adult chases them. Anyone who gets tagged by the adult before reaching the line becomes a helper and stands behind the adult line in the next round. Continue playing until all kids have been caught.

Mexican Treasure Hunt There's a treasure for each child hidden in Mexico (a certain area of your house or yard marked off with a string or streamer as a borderline), but the children need passports to cross the border. The guests decorate index card passports with stickers, washable markers or crayons, magazine pictures, photos, glue sticks, and fingerprints using an inkpad. Laminate the passports by covering them with clear contact paper. When the kids present their passports at the border, they receive an empty treasure chest (use plastic diaper wipe boxes or shoeboxes). At parties for older children, you may also hand out treasure maps marked with the locations of hidden treasures. The children will find several baskets hidden in Mexico, each stocked with one party favor for each guest.

Gatos y Perros Identify one or two guests to be the Perros (dogs). The remaining guests will be the Gatos (cats). The Perros chase the Gatos within a designated area, such as a driveway. When a Gato is tagged, she must freeze in place. Other Gatos may "thaw" frozen Gatos by crawling through their legs. Once a Gato has been tagged three times, she becomes a Perro. The last remaining Gato is the winner and begins the next round by being the first Perro.

Piñata Buy a traditional donkey piñata at a party goods store, or make a Piñata with a gift bag. Cut off the bottom and then reattach it loosely with tape. Fill it with candy and small toys. Hang it from the ceiling or a tree from the handles. Decorate it with red, orange, and yellow streamers and balloons.

Taco Time Give each guest a couple of empty taco shells and set up individual bowls of cooked hamburger, lettuce, tomato, cheese, and condiments (sour cream, guacamole, salsa). Let the kids make their own tacos.

Decorations

Put a sombrero on a table with tortilla chips in the rim (look at a party goods store for an inexpensive sombrero or a plastic sombrero-shaped chip'n'dip platter), play recorded guitar music, drape colorful Southwestern blankets around the party room, and place other Mexican-theme objects around the room, such as clay pots or cactus plants.

Cake

Write "Feliz Cumpleanos" on the cake instead of Happy Birthday. Use red, yellow, and orange frosting to create the image of falling confetti and spiraling streamers on the cake. Serve lime slushes made from mixing a can of frozen limeade, one can of water, and ice in a blender.

Party Favors

Real Mexican coins
Mini cactus plants
Chocolate gold coins
Mexican jumping beans
Mini sombreros

Medieval Party

Engage children in this royal fantasy party of lords and ladies,
princes and princesses, and kings and queens.
Ages: 4 to 7

Invitations

Cut construction paper into the shape of a castle and glue it to the front of a folded piece of heavyweight paper. The birthday child can decorate the castle with glitter glue, markers, and stickers. Write, "The House of Merrigan cordially invites you to the enchanted land of Framingham for the royal birthday celebration of Lord Quinn" (or Lady Elizabeth) on the outside and include the party details inside.

Activities

Announce the Guests As the children arrive, give them cardboard tubes from wrapping paper. Let them "trumpet" guests who arrive subsequently, and announce their names, inserting a "Lord" or "Lady" before their first names. If the celebration will be held outdoors, give each guest a small cup of "outdoor confetti" (actually grass seed or birdseed) and let them toss the confetti at the arriving guests.

Encrusted Party Hat Decorating Purchase solid-colored birthday hats. For the girls' hats, pull a strip of gauzy material through the tip of birthday hats to hang down from the top, and tape the end to the inside of the hat so it will stay secure. (You may need to cut the tips off the birthday hats for the gauze to fit through.) At the party, lay out the birthday hats, fake jewels, stickers, miniature cocktail swords, tape, and glue sticks. Let the guests decorate their royal party hats.

Castle Building Before the party, cut a door and windows out of a huge appliance box. At the party, give the kids the appliance box, washable paints, paintbrushes, markers, magazine photos, and glue sticks and have them decorate the box to look like a castle. If you've invited more than six or eight guests, then consider using two or more appliance boxes.

Medieval Dress Up For the girls, gather princess dress-up clothes or ask guests to come dressed as princesses. Lay out strands of beads, rings, earrings, ribbons, high heels, hair accessories, and so on for them to complete the look. The boys can decorate armor chest shields with stickers and markers and label them with their knight names, such as Sir Zachary. To make the shields before the party, cut poster board into a shield shape and thread a piece of rope through the middle for holding on to the shield. Give the boys wrapping paper rolls to represent swords (you might spray paint these silver before the party) and lay out dress-up clothes like capes, tunics, hats, and crowns. Let them engage in some friendly jousting in the courtyard outside their castle.

Set a rule that their swords may only touch other weapons, not kids. Take instant photos of all the guests and give these as party favors.

Horse Race Gather a few horses on sticks, or use brooms and other household objects as pretend horses. Let the guests take turns racing each other from a start line to a finish line on their horses. Everyone wins a party favor at the finish line. At parties for kids who are 6 years old and older, hold a horse relay race, where the guests are divided into two teams that race against each other.

Enchanted Forest Before the party, create an Enchanted Forest in an area of your home or yard. If it's inside, bring in large branches and hang them from the ceiling and lean them against the walls. Wrap fake ivy through the dry branches and scatter bird ornaments and leaves throughout. Move all your houseplants to this area to add to the forest feel. You could create a similar area outside. Wrap a small party favor for each guest, each in a different kind of wrapping paper (use any kind of wrapping paper you have on hand, such as the comics from the Sunday paper, Christmas paper, baby shower paper, etc.). Also cut a small square of each wrapping paper and put the squares in a bowl. Hide each gift in the Enchanted Forest, nestling them between the branches. At the party, each child draws a square of wrapping paper from the bowl. They then go to the Enchanted Forest to find the gift with the matching wrapping paper.

Dodge Ball (ages 6 and up) Use a soft ball about the size of a volleyball and play this game in the courtyard of the castle. Split the kids into two teams. One team makes a circle and the other team stands inside. The team that formed the circle takes turns throwing the ball at the kids inside the circle. When a child is hit by the ball, then he joins the team forming the circle. The last kid left inside the circle wins a medieval gold coin (actually a chocolate gold coin). Play again, and let the teams switch starting positions.

Piñata Create a Medieval piñata by cutting the bottom out of a gift bag, then loosely taping it back in place. Place some candy and confetti in the bottom of the bag, tape it closed, and decorate it with purple ribbons, streamers, and ivy. Run string through the handles and hang it in the party room or from a tree branch outside.

Decorations

Employ a purple and gold color scheme to transform the party room into a royal castle. Use purple tablecloths, plates, napkins, and cups, and toss some gold chocolate coins in the center of each table. Create a throne for the birthday child by draping a chair with branches, leaves, fake ivy, and streamers.

Cake

Use a cake mix to make two square cakes (8" or 9"). Once cooled, place one layer down on the cake plate and frost it. Cut a 4" square out of the center of the other layer and lay the remaining cake on top and frost it. Cut the 4" square into four 2" squares and place each of these on a corner of the cake and frost them. Place inverted sugar cones on top of each 2" square and frost these. Add miniature flags to the tops of the cones, and add candies around the bottom of the cones and all around the cake. Stick a sugar wafer cookie onto the side of the cake for a door, and add a few rectangular cookies or bars to create a ramp leading to the door. Add swords and figurines of princesses, knights, and horses to the cake and the plate. Serve the cake without utensils, and explain that the medieval custom was to eat with your hands. Make miniature fruit kabobs by piercing pieces of fruit with miniature swords.

Party Favors

Be sure to label the party favor bags with titled names, such as "Lord Christopher" and "Lady Jacqueline"

Gold chocolate coins
Jewelry
Fake jewels
Coloring books
Stickers
Decorated party hats and armor shields

Cinderella Party

This timeless classic is a great choice for a party theme because everyone knows the story of Cinderella. Children will especially enjoy the role-playing game at this party.

Ages: 4 to 8

Invitations

Use a home computer to print royal-looking invitations with fancy lettering. Start with, "The Prince is throwing a Cinderella ball to celebrate Katie's 5th birthday!" and then list the party details. If the invitations are being hand-delivered, roll them up scroll-style and tie them with a ribbon.

Activities

Cinderella's Magic Dust As guests arrive at the party, welcome them with a shower of magic dust—actually confetti. Give each guest a small cup filled with confetti for throwing.

Slipper Cookies Before the party, make a batch of cookies in the shape of Cinderella's glass slipper using cookie cutters or a stencil. Lay the cookies out along with a variety of pastel-colored frosting and iridescent candies. As the guests arrive, let them each decorate their own slipper cookie.

Royal Masks Set out solid-colored half-face masks, glue sticks, stickers, colored feathers, and craft "jewels." Let the kids each decorate a mask to wear to the ball.

Cinderella's Slipper Hunt To prepare for this hunt, get a flashy pair of women's shoes or slippers, hide both shoes, and create two different sets of clues, each leading to one of the hidden slippers. Get two different colors of paper and write the clues on the paper—one set of clues on one color paper and the other set on the other color. The clues should lead the kids from the location of one clue to the next, and the final clue in each set will lead kids to a hidden slipper. Split the kids into teams by drawing two different colors of candies out of a hat, and give each team their first clue. Once each team finds their hidden slipper, they turn it in for a special prize for each team member. If the kids are too young to read, the clues can be drawings or instant photos of where to find the next clue, rather than a worded description. For 4-year-olds, you may simply hide several shoes and slippers throughout the room or yard, ask them to pick up as many as they can find, and reward them with a gold chocolate coin for each slipper found.

Going to the Ball In this game, an adult acts like the evil stepmother and gives each guest a broom or a dusting rag for them to use to clean the party room before they can go to the ball. They must pick up all the confetti on the floor from the Confetti Throw! Once the room is cleaned to the evil stepmother's satisfaction, the guests may dress up for the ball. Provide crowns, jewelry, scarves, gloves, and other dress-up clothes.

Freeze Dancing at the Ball Once the guests are all dressed up, play some bouncy music for dancing. When the music stops, they must freeze in place.

Cinderella's Slipper Race Establish a starting line and a finish line. Each guest must remove one shoe and put it into a big pile at the finish line. At "Go!" the guests run to the finish line, find their own shoe, put it on, and run back to the starting line, where they all win a prize for completing the race. Weather and space permitting, you can make this race more challenging by having guests run around a tree, a chair, or the house, once both their shoes are on. At parties for older children, have a slipper relay race, where the children are divided into teams, and the teams race to find their shoes one guest at a time.

Midnight This outdoor game will help the kids remember what time Cinderella needs to be home. Establish two lines that are at least twenty or thirty yards apart. You may use sidewalk chalk on a driveway to draw the lines, or identify markers as boundaries. Kids line up behind one line, while an adult stands behind the other line. The adult yells a time, such as "Two o'clock", and the kids take steps towards the adult—one step for each hour on the clock (for example, the kids all take two steps for two o'clock). The adult continues calling times, and the kids keep stepping toward the adult's line. When the adult yells midnight, the guests must run back to their line for safety while the adult chases them. Anyone who gets tagged by the adult before reaching the line becomes a helper and stands behind the adult line in the next round. Continue playing until all kids have been caught.

Decorations

Get out your pumpkin decorations and add pink and blue balloons and streamers. Create a special throne for the birthday girl and give her a tiara to wear instead of a birthday hat.

Cake

Serve orange-frosted cupcakes decorated with candies to look like pumpkin faces. Serve with "pumpkin punch" (actually orange flavored punch.) After the birthday girl blows out the candles, give the guests more magic dust (confetti) to toss at her.

Party Favors

Cinderella coloring books
Miniature Cinderella books
Stickers
Miniature pumpkins
Pumpkin candy
Tiaras
Costume jewelry

Wild West Party

Recreate the adventure and fun of the wild, wild, west at this exciting party.
Ages: 4 to 8

Invitations

Create an invitation that looks like an old-fashioned wanted poster. Use a headline such as, "Wanted! Matthew's Friends!" and list the party details below.

Activities

Cowboy Boot Decorating Before the party, cut several large cowboy boots out of construction paper. Set these shapes out along with glitter glue, jewels, markers, and hole punchers and let the guests decorate their cowboy boots.

Cowboy Dress-up Lay out several cowboy items, such as sheriff badges, bandannas, cowboy hats, boots, and holsters. The kids dress up as cowboys, then an adult takes a picture with an instant camera, if one is available.

Pony Rides Arrange for a local stable to bring a pony or two to your home and take each guest on a short pony ride. This can begin while kids are dressing up as cowboys, so some guests can continue to dress up while others are riding the pony.

Pony Express (ages 6 and up) Split the kids into two teams. Have each team stand in a line. Give the leader of each team an envelope. At "Go!" the leader passes the envelope to the next person in line, who passes it to the next one, and so on, until the last guest in line has the envelope. The last guest then runs to the front of the line and the team passes the envelope down again, and the last person runs to the front. The first team to get the leader at the front of the line again wins.

Outlaw Relay Race (ages 5 and up) Before the party, place two black outlaw outfits (black hat, shirt, and pants) into two bags or suitcases. Split the kids into two teams, and have them stand behind the starting line. The first child in each team must run to the suitcase, put on the outlaw outfit over his clothes, and run back to the team, leaving the suitcase in its place. The outfit is then removed (the other kids on the team can help), and the next child in line puts on the outlaw outfit and runs around the suitcase. The next child puts on the outfit, and so on. The last team member must run back to the suitcase and put the outlaw outfit back inside. The first team to have the outfit back into the suitcase wins. If you have a video camera, it's worth it to videotape this game and then play it back while the kids are eating cake, especially if you can play it backwards or in fast motion.

Sheriff Chase Toss several dozen pennies or gold coins on the ground on one side of the driveway. Put an empty bowl on the other side. The guests, playing the role of outlaws, must pick up the coins one at a time, carry them across the driveway, and deposit them into the bowl. As they're doing this, the sheriff (played by an adult) is in the driveway chasing down the outlaws. Any outlaw who is tagged by the sheriff must turn over the coin to the sheriff. The outlaws continue playing the game until all the coins are in the bowl, then they split what they've collected.

Panning for Gold Before the party, create gold nuggets by painting small stones with gold spray paint. Hide these in a designated area of the house or yard and give the children pans or plastic bags and instruct them to collect as many nuggets of gold as they can. At parties for older children, you may use a permanent marker to write weights on each nugget. After all the nuggets have been found, guests each count their nuggets and add up their weights. They earn special prizes for collecting the highest total weight, the lightest nugget, the highest number of nuggets, and so on.

Decorations

See if your local post office will give you any old wanted posters, or make some of your own on your computer. Create a covered wagon by placing some pillows in a wagon and covering them with a sheet. Scatter haystacks, hoes, cowboy boots, and cowboy hats around the party room. Label the party room with a sign that says "The OK Corral." Use a plaid or checked tablecloth on the party table, and decorate the table with hay and figurines of horses and cowboys.

Cake

Create a Wild West scene on the top of a sheet cake. Build a corral around the outside of the cake using thin pretzel sticks. Inside the corral, place small plastic toys such as horses, covered wagons, and cowboys. Make a dirt trail on top of the cake using brown sugar or crushed chocolate wafer cookies.

Party Favors

Gold candy nuggets
Instant photos
Gold coins
Bandannas
Sheriff badges
Wanted posters
Dress-up items

Garden Party

This party is an ideal celebration for the child who loves nature and gardening.
Ages: 4 to 8

Invitations

Fold a piece of heavyweight paper in half. Glue or tape a few flower and vegetable seeds to the front cover and have the birthday child draw some flowers and vegetables sprouting from the seeds. Write the party information inside.

Activities

Garden Pot Kids decorate a clay flowerpot with paint, ribbon, fabric, and glue.

Garden Gloves Guests decorate garden gloves with fabric paint, adhesive jewels, lace, fabric, beads, and glue.

Flower Treasure Hunt Before the party, cut several pictures of flowers out of a gardening catalog or magazine. Make two photocopies of each one, and hide the photocopies. At the party, each guest blindly selects a flower picture out of a bowl. Guests must then find the two matching flower pictures in the designated area of the house or yard, and then turn in all three pictures for a party favor. Guests who can identify the name of their flower win an extra prize. At parties with older children, you may make this game more challenging by writing clues on the back of each flower picture that hint at the location of another matching picture. For pre-readers, the clues may be hand-drawn pictures of the hiding spots of the matching flower pictures.

Flower Memory Game Fill a tray with ten to fifteen objects related to flowers—a gardening tool, a seed, a bulb, a fake flower, a gardening glove, a flower pot, a dishtowel with flowers, a book about flowers, and so on. Cover the tray with a towel. Have the guests sit in a circle. Remove the towel and let them stare at the tray for a minute or two as you review all the items on the tray. Put the towel back over the tray, then go around the circle. One at a time, each guest tries to remember something on the tray. Correct guesses are awarded with a sticker or a piece of candy. At parties for older children, guests are given paper and a pencil and are asked to write down as many items from the tray as they can remember.

Pressed Flower Bookmarks or Placemats Set out several colorful gardening catalogs with lots of photos, scissors, glue sticks, markers, and construction paper cut into strips the size of bookmarks. The kids then cut out pictures of flowers and glue them to the construction paper using the glue stick. They may also decorate their bookmarks with markers or stickers. An adult helps by applying clear contact paper to the bookmarks and helping the kids trim around the edges. The same can be done using whole sheets of construction paper to create placemats.

Gardener's Price is Right Gather at least five party favors related to the gardening theme, such as a packet of seeds, a small gardening tool, or a small notebook with a flower on the cover. Line the party favors up on a table. Write the price of each favor on a slip of paper and place the price facedown behind the favor. Give each guest a piece of paper and pencil. One by one, hold up each favor, describe it, and ask guests to write down their guess of the price. The partygoer with the guess that's closest to the actual price (without going over the actual price) wins that party favor.

Planting After the paint on the clay pots is dry to the touch, set out several small flowering plants, fertilizer, and soil and have each child plant a flower in his or her pot.

Decorations

Put a lacy tablecloth on the dining table. Put out nice dinnerware and doilies and place potted flowers and cut flowers in vases throughout the room and on the table. Hang strands of Christmas lights. If the weather's nice, set up the table outside in a real garden.

Cake

Make chocolate pudding and pour it into clear plastic cups or mini-clay pots that have been lined with foil. Spread a layer of crushed Oreos on top, stick a fake flower into the pot, and lay a gummy worm on the dirt.

Party Favors

Decorated garden gloves
Decorated clay pots with planted flowers
Mini watering cans
Packets of seeds
Anything with a flower pattern (pencils, mini notebooks, stickers)

All-American Bike Party

If your child seems to prefer riding a bike to most other activities,
a bike party is an ideal celebration!

Ages: 4 to 8

Invitations

Cut a diamond shape out of heavyweight yellow paper and outline it with a black marker. Write, "Caution! Bike on Over to Madison's All-American Birthday Party!" on one side and write the party details on the back. Add flag stickers to both sides of the invitation. Ask guests to bring their bikes to the party.

Activities

Vanity License Plates Before the party, cut red, white, and blue poster board into the size of a license plate that will hang beneath a bike seat. Outline the shape with a permanent marker and punch two holes in the top. Lay out the license plates, glitter glue, markers, paints, stickers, and ribbon or string, and let the guests create their own patriotic license plates and hang them from their bike seats. You may use clear contact paper to laminate the license plates.

Bike Decorating Set out red, white, and blue streamers, baseball cards, feathers, pipe cleaners, pom-poms, clothespins, tin cans, plastic bottles, bike beads, ribbons, and other items for the kids to use to decorate their bikes.

Bike Parade Once the bikes are all decorated, have the children line up and parade down the street or driveway. Award prizes for the "Most Colorful Bike," the "Most Festive Bike," the "Most Decorated Bike," the "Simplest Bike," the "Biggest Bike," the "Newest Bike," the "Fastest Bike," the "Most Patriotic Bike," and so on.

Bike Obstacle Course Before the party, enlist the help of the birthday child to set up an age-appropriate bicycle obstacle course in your driveway or street for the kids to race through on their bikes. Let them each try it a couple of times. At parties for older kids, time the racers and award a prize to the fastest biker.

Bike Relay Race (ages 6 and up) Split the guests into two teams. Establish a starting line and a finish line using sidewalk chalk. Give each team a mitten or glove. The first rider in each team puts the glove on his hand, rides his bike to the finish line, turns around, and rides back to the starting line. He hands the glove off to the next guest in line, who puts it on her hand, rides her bike to the finish line and back, and then hands the glove off to the next guest in line. Continue until everyone's had a chance to ride. The first team to finish wins.

Decorations

Use poster board or foam core to create traffic signs to post around the party room or yard. Yellow diamond-shaped signs may read, "Caution, It's Madison's Birthday!" "Caution, Kids Having Fun" and "Caution, Madison is 6!" Red hexagon signs may read, "STOP and say Happy Birthday to Madison" "STOP eating all the cake!" and "STOP falling off your bike!" Play up the patriotic theme by decorating with flags and red, white, and blue streamers. Use paper goods from Independence Day.

Cake

Create a bike profile cake by baking two round cakes and setting them next to each other. Make the cakes look like wheels by using icing to create spokes. Use licorice for the bike frame and handlebars. Line up gumdrops, wafer cookies, or other candy to create the seat.

Party Favors

Bike accessories
Water bottles
Whistles
Baseball cards
Bike stickers
Bike beads
Wrist sweatbands

Victorian Tea Party

*Tea, treasures, and straw hat decorating are all part of
this old-fashioned tea party celebration.*
Ages: 4 to 8

Invitations

Create teapot-shaped invitations using colored paper. Write, "Don't be late!
It's a very important date! It's Alicia's Victorian Tea Party!" on the front.
Decorate it with flower stickers or dot flowers, which are created by dipping
the flat eraser of a pencil into paints and dabbing several dots on to the page
to resemble a circle of petals, and then dabbing a dot of a different color for
the center of the flower. The party information can be written on the back.
Ask the guests to dress up for tea.

Activities

Mad Hatter Straw Hat Decorating The partygoers adorn the rims of
straw hats with flowers and colorful buttons. Visit a craft store or a discount

store to purchase straw hats, small wired flowers, ribbon, large colorful buttons, and other decorative accessories. You can also spray paint small puzzle pieces for the hats. Lay out all the accessories along with craft wire and masking tape. Show the guests how to tie the ribbon around the rim of the hats and then insert and secure the flowers and buttons into the rim using the craft wire and masking tape. An adult can use a glue gun to attach ribbon to each hat. As an alternative, you may offer gender-neutral hats and decorations such as buttons, puzzle pieces, and beaded safety pins.

Craft Stations Set up a few stations for the guests to rotate among. Hire a helper (a high schooler would be great) to paint flowers, polka dots, or stripes on the guests' fingernails using nail polish. Set up a hair beading station where guests each have a tiny strand of hair braided and decorated with a stack of beads held in place by a rubber band at the bottom. At the safety pin beading station, provide several different kinds of beads and different sizes of safety pins and let guests string beads onto the safety pins, hang a few beaded pins off a large one, and pin them onto their clothes, shoelaces, backpacks, or hats. At parties for older children, you may set up a station for making friendship bracelets.

Teabag Hunt It's time for tea, but the teabags are missing! Before the party, hide a few dozen tea bags around the party room or yard. Let the guests pick up as many as they can find and then exchange each one for a party favor, such as a gold chocolate coin or a sticker. For older guests, you can make it more challenging by assigning different point values to the tea bags based on the color of their tag.

Treasure Teapot Place several party favors in a teapot, so there are at least two or three for each guest. Have the children sit on the floor in a circle while you play music. When the music stops, the guest may reach into the teapot without looking and pull out a party favor. Continue playing until the teapot is empty.

Tea Time Present a snack of tea and crumpets. Use cookie cutters to create heart- and star-shaped finger sandwiches. Serve a couple of different fruity flavors of lukewarm decaffeinated tea along with sugar cubes and cream. When it's time to serve the cake, pretend that you've just found it missing, and that you need the help of the guests to find it, as described in the following activity.

Teapot Cake Hunt (ages 5 and up) Now the birthday cake is missing! The culprit has left a trail of clues to help the guests find the cake. (Before the party, you've hidden the cake in the bathtub.) Create a series of at least ten clues leading to the cake's hiding spot. Fold each clue in half and label the outside with a guest's name. There should be enough clues so that each guest will have at least one. Each clue is a description of where to find the next clue, and it can be a drawing, an instant photo, a clip-art illustration, or words—depending on the age and sophistication of the children. Give the first clue in the series to the birthday child inside a balloon that must be popped. The group will then find the next clue, which will have a name on it. The person named can open the clue. Together, the group finds the next clue, and the person named can open it. Continue until they've found the cake, and then carefully bring it into the tea salon and serve it. At parties for younger children, adults will need to provide coaching and help throughout the treasure hunt. If your child's celebration includes more than eight guests, then consider developing two different sets of clues, each on a different color paper, and each following an entirely different trail, but leading to the same end. Split the party into two groups and have them race to find the hidden cake.

Decorations

Cover the party table with a floor-length tablecloth. Add some flowers in vases, toss some pastel-colored tissue-paper confetti or crinkle paper on the table, and add a miniature tea set if you have one. Set each place setting with a doily, a couple of pretty plates set on top of each other, a teacup and saucer, silverware, and a pretty napkin. Cloth napkins in napkin rings and nice dishes are sure to impress the guests, if you're up for the extra work and the risk of breakage. Place a pair of white gloves at each place setting and ask the guests to wear them for tea, along with their straw hats.

Cake

Create an impressive teapot cake by making two cake mixes and baking each in a 1.5 quart ovenproof bowl for about 55 minutes. Remove the cakes from the bowls and cut a one-inch slice off the bottom of one of the cakes. Stack the two cakes on top of each other to form the body of the teapot, starting with the cake with the slice removed (bottom side down) and then adding the other one (bottom side up). The one-inch slice will be the teapot cover, so place it on top. Frost the three layers together and frost the entire cake. Add a gumdrop to the very top, and form a handle and spout from play-dough and attach those to the cake using toothpicks. Decorate the teapot with flower designs made from candy dots, and add a circle of candy dots around the cover. Before cutting the cake, separate the two large layers and remove the play-dough.

Party Favors

If you can find several old-fashioned purses at a thrift shop, you can give these as party favors and place other favors inside.

Teacups
Sachets
White gloves
Decorated straw hats
Beaded pins
Dress-up jewelry

Fun in the Sun Party

This active outdoor celebration is great fun on a warm, sunny day!
Ages: 4 to 8

Invitations

Make watermelon invitations by cutting deep pink paper into a large circle and outlining the outer edge with a green marker. Cut the circle into quarters (four slices of watermelon) and add seeds with a black permanent marker to make it look like a slice of watermelon. On the front write, "Come Have Some Fun in the Sun at Joseph's Birthday Party!" Write the party details on the back. Ask kids to bring their bathing suits and a towel. Decorate the outside of the envelope with sun stickers. Consider setting a rain date or having an alternate party ready in case of inclement weather.

Activities

Crossfire This noncompetitive warm-up game is ideal to play across a driveway. Split the children into two teams. One team stands on one side of the driveway, and the other team stands on the other side. The birthday child is "it" in the first round and stands in the center of the driveway. When "it" calls "Run!" the children on both sides of the driveway run to the other side of the driveway while "it" tries to tag them. Anyone who gets tagged joins "it" in the center of the driveway for the next round and helps "it" tag the other children. Keep playing until there's only one runner left. That player becomes "it" in the next round. Run a couple of sprinklers on either side of the driveway and tell the kids to avoid getting wet while playing this game.

Water Obstacle Course Set up an obstacle course through sprinklers. Kids try to run through the obstacle course without getting wet. If the kids are older, time them running through the course and award a prize to the partygoer with the fastest time.

Slip and Slide Spread out a plastic lawn slide and wet it down. Let the kids take turns sliding on it and give prizes for the longest tummy slide, the longest back slide, the craziest slide, and so on.

Water Balloon Toss Two guests stand several feet apart and throw a water balloon back and forth to each other. When one drops the water balloon and it breaks, another child replaces him. When one player in that pair drops a water balloon, then another child replaces her. Continue playing until all but one child has been eliminated.

Hose Limbo Prop a hose up on a picnic table by squeezing it through the boards of the table. Point the hose upward so that the water sprays up into the air. Guests take turns doing the limbo under the water spray without getting wet. Keep lowering the level of the water spray until everyone's been eliminated.

Water Balloon Dodge Ball Split the kids into two teams. One team makes a circle, and the other team stands inside. The team that formed the circle takes turns throwing water balloons at the kids inside the circle. When a child gets soaked by a water balloon, then he or she joins the team forming the outer circle. The last kid left inside the circle wins a special prize. Play again, and have the teams switch starting positions. The noncompetitive version of this game has successful thrower replacing the person she hit.

Red Rover Split the kids into two teams and have each team stand in a line, holding hands and facing the other line. The lines should be several feet apart. One team begins by yelling, "Red Rover, Red Rover, send Jonathan right over!" The child on the other team whose name was called runs over and tries to break through the line. If he's successful, then he returns to his line. If he doesn't break through the line, then he stays with the new team. The opposite team then calls a guest over. Keep playing until all the kids are on the same team.

Sunny Treasure Hunt Get several different colors of paper, one for each guest. Cut a circle shape out of each color using zigzag scissors. Cut each sun shape into three pieces. Place one of the pieces in a resealable plastic bag along with a piece of candy and bury it in the sandbox or hide it in the yard. Place another piece in a resealable plastic bag along with another piece of candy and place it in a children's wading pool that's filled with water. Place the third piece of each sun in a large bowl. At the party, the kids each draw a piece of a sun out of a bowl, then try to find their matching pieces in the sandbox and pool. Once they've found all three pieces, they can trade them in for a party favor.

Decorations

Create a huge sun banner by cutting a sun shape out of a large, yellow, paper tablecloth and gluing it to a white, paper tablecloth. Add birthday greetings such as "Happy Birthday, Joseph!" "Fun in the Sun!" and "Now You're 7!" and hang it in a prominent spot outdoors. Purchase solid yellow balloons, streamers, and paper goods. Use a black peremanent marker to draw sun shapes on the balloons.

Cake

Make a round cake and decorate it with bright yellow frosting to look like the sun. Create pointy rays from poster board and stick them into the sides of the cake.

Party Favors

Sunglasses
Water bottles
Squirt guns
Bubbles
Frisbees
Sidewalk chalk

Baby Party

*Young children who are fascinated with babies and love playing
with baby dolls will enjoy this party that celebrates new life.*
Ages: 4 to 8

Invitations

Purchase stationary or invitations normally used for baby showers. Write, "You're invited to Kaelyn's BABY birthday party!" Ask guests to bring their favorite baby doll to the party.

Activities

Welcome Nap Time Before the party, ask the birthday child to set up a nap area for all the visiting babies. This may include doll beds, strollers, and baby blankets. As guests arrive with their baby dolls, ask them to find a snuggly napping spot for their babies to sleep while they join the party.

Birth Certificates Take an instant photo of each guest with her baby doll and staple these to birth certificate forms that you've created before the party. The birth certificate can ask questions such as: Baby's Name, Mother's Name, Age, Eye Color (provide multiple choice), Hair Color (provide multiple choice), Length (provide measuring tape), and Baby's Favorite Color. Adults can help complete the birth certificates for young children, but older guests will enjoy doing it themselves. Leave a space for the guests to draw a picture of their babies, and provide stickers of rattles, footprints, and bottles for guests to use in decorating their birth certificates.

Shrinky Dinks Guests use colored pencils to trace and color images onto clear plastic Shrinky Dinks sheets. They cut out the drawings, and an adult punches a hole in the image and bakes it in the oven for a couple of minutes. As they're baked, the Shrinky Dinks magically shrink to one-third their original size and become nine times thicker. Once the images are shrunk, guests can string their designs onto yarn to make necklaces for their baby dolls. Provide guests with images for tracing that are related to babies, such as bottles, rattles, carriages, and blocks. You can purchase *The Shrinky Dinks Book* and Shrinky Dinks refill pack from www.amazon.com or your local bookstore.

Meet the Babies Guests sit on the floor in a circle with their babies and act out conversations that moms have at the playground by introducing themselves and their babies to the group. Rotate introductions around the circle and ask each guest to provide one fact about her baby, such as the baby's age.

Baby Care Buy a package of small diapers for premature babies and give each guest a diaper, a hand towel, a diaper wipe, and other baby grooming supplies. Lead the guests by demonstrating how to change a diaper and groom babies.

Counting Contest Fill a baby food jar with pastel jelly beans, gum balls, or other small candies. Ask guests to guess how many candies are in the jar and write their guess on a slip of paper. The closest guess wins the jar, and the winner is asked to give a candy to each of the other guests.

Baby Memory Tray Place at least a dozen baby objects on a tray, such as a pacifier, a diaper, a baby book, a baby jar, a teething ring, a rattle, a baby blanket, a baby toy, baby powder, baby lotion, baby shoes, baby shampoo, a baby spoon, a block, and a baby comb. Cover the tray with a towel. As the guests sit on the floor in a circle, unveil the tray and point out each object on the tray. Then remove the tray and split the guests into pairs. Give each pair a paper and a pencil and ask them to write down as many baby objects from the tray as they can remember. Give the winning team a prize and the other teams a consolation prize. If some guests cannot write yet, be sure to pair them with guests who can. (As an alternative, guests take turns naming one object from the tray. Start with the birthday child and move clockwise around the circle. The last guest to remember an object wins a small prize.) At the end, unveil the tray again to remind guests of all the objects on the tray.

Baby Toy Relay Race Split the guests into two teams and establish a starting line and a goal line. At the goal line, place two sets of the stacking cups baby toy. The first guest in each line runs to the stacking cups and carries the largest cup back to the line. The second guest in line takes the largest cup back to the goal line, inverts it, picks up the next largest cup, inverts it, and places it on top of the largest cup. This guest must run back to the line while balancing these two cups on one another without dropping either one. Guests continue adding an inverted cup to the top of the stack. If a guest drops a cup, the team must start over with the largest cup. The first team to successfully bring the entire tower of stacking cups back to the starting line wins.

Baby Food Taste Test Give each player a baby spoon and let her sample three different jars of baby food, labeled #1, #2, and #3, and guess what type of baby food is in each jar.

Pass the Present Before the party, find a series of boxes that nest inside each other. In the smallest box, place a small party favor for each guest, such as a candy pacifier. Wrap this box with baby shower paper and then place the wrapped present in the next biggest box. Wrap this with baby shower paper, and keep going until the largest box is wrapped. At the party, play music as the kids pass the present from one child to the next. When the music stops, the child holding the box opens it. If it's another wrapped box, start the music, and the box gets passed again. Keep going until the final box is opened, and then each child gets a favor from the smallest box.

Decorations

Use any baby shower decorations you may have to decorate the party room. You may also fill baby bottles with shredded paper in festive colors and hang these around the room and place them on the table. Post a few photos of the birthday child as baby, and decorate with pink and blue streamers. Hang a clothesline in the party room and pin baby clothes to it.

Cake

Decorate a layer cake with light pink and blue frosting and baby shower favors such as plastic baby blocks, plastic baby shoes, or a pretend pacifier. Use pink and blue candles and serve the cake with baby spoons.

Party Favors

Candy pacifiers or ring pops

Baby food jars filled with snacks such as crackers or cereal and decorated
with baby stickers and festive ribbon

Baby sleeping bags (if you're handy with a sewing machine, create simple
rectangular sleeping bags for babies)

Shrinky Dink necklaces created at the party

Baby toys

Baby spoons

Costume Party

Kids of all ages love dressing up. The birthday child may customize this party by selecting a central theme for the costumes such as cartoon characters, Bible heroes, or characters from a favorite book or movie.

Ages: 4 to 8

Invitations

Fold a heavyweight piece of white paper in half. On the top half of the outside cover, write, "You're Invited to Shawna's Bible Hero Party!" Use invisible ink to write a secret message underneath this by dipping a toothpick into lemon juice. Use it as a pen to write "Come dressed as your favorite Bible hero!" Draw a box around the invisible message. When a flame is held near this message, it will become visible. On the inside of the invitation, provide the party details and tell guests to get help from a parent to reveal the secret message in the box by holding it over a burning candle.

Activities

Masquerade Masks Set out colorful masquerade masks along with glitter glue, glittery confetti, and craft jewels. (These masks and other supplies are available from Oriental Trading Company at oriental.com.) As guests arrive, they create masks to complement their costumes.

Character ID Card Take an instant photo of guests as they arrive at the party in costume. Staple this to a large index card that guests can decorate and complete with key information about their characters or heroes. You may create blank forms that include questions such as hero/character name, birthplace, what makes the hero heroic, hero's friends, and so on. Children who are too young to write words may enjoy drawing pictures of their hero or character in action and decorating the ID card with stickers and glitter glue.

Egg Heads A couple weeks before the party, fill empty egg shell halves with soil and plant some grass seeds in the soil. Place the egg shell halves in small bathroom cups so they won't roll over. Place the cups on the windowsill and let the grass grow. At the party, give guests markers, wiggly eyes, and glitter glue to create faces on the egg shell. Encourage guests to create faces that look like the faces of their dress-up characters.

Circle of Characters Set up a circle of chairs facing out. There should be one less chair than the number of guests. An adult records the name of each character or hero on a slip of paper and puts the slips in a bowl. The adult also includes a slip of paper that says "everyone." Guests sit in the chairs while the birthday child pulls a slip of paper out of the bowl and calls out the name. The guest(s) dressed as this character must get up from his chair, run around the circle clockwise, and try to sit back in the same chair or any other chair that has been vacated. Guests must run around the full circle at least once before sitting. At the same time that the guests are racing to get back to their seats, the birthday child races to sit in an open seat. The first person to reach the open chair sits in it in the next round. The person left without a chair pulls the next name out of the bowl in the next round. Be ready for mass confusion when "everyone" is pulled!

Memory Tray Place at least a dozen objects that are related to your party theme on a tray. For example, if the dress-up theme is a movie about jungle characters, items on the tray may include a book about the jungle, the movie video box, stuffed jungle animals, an animal sticker, and so on. Birthday party items such as a candle, balloon, noisemaker, or bow may also be included. If the theme is Bible heroes, items on the tray could include five small stones (like David used to fight Goliath), a whale toy (a reminder of the big fish that swallowed Jonah), a toy trumpet (like the ones used by Joshua and the Israelites in the Battle of Jericho), a stuffed lion (a reminder of Daniel in the lions' den), and a pair of matching stuffed animals (like the animals Noah took onto the ark). Cover the tray with a towel. As the guests sit on the floor in a circle, unveil the tray and point out each object on the tray. Then remove the tray and split the guests into pairs. Give each pair some paper and a pencil and ask them to write down as many objects from the tray as they can remember. Give the winning team a prize and the other teams a consolation prize. If some guests cannot write yet, be sure to pair them with guests who can. (As an alternative, guests take turns naming one object from the tray out loud. Start with the birthday child and move clockwise around the circle. The last guest to remember an object wins a small prize.) At the end, unveil the tray again to remind guests of all the objects on the tray.

Character Walk Before the party, identify about five or six character names or Bible hero names and write them on paper plates, one name per plate. You should have as many plates as guests at the party. Arrange the plates in a large circle on the floor. At the party, play theme-related music as the guests walk around the circle, stepping from plate to plate. When the music stops, each child stands on a plate, and an adult pulls a character name from a bowl. The children standing on plates with the name called win a small prize, such as a piece of candy. Keep playing until every guest has won at least one prize. To make things move faster, you can draw two names from the bowl on each round.

Huckle Buckle Beanstalk Before the party, the birthday child selects a theme-related toy or figurine that fits into the palm of his hand. The birthday child shows the guests the toy, then hides it in the party room while all the guests are waiting in another room. He must hide it in a location that is visible without moving any objects in the room. Once the toy is hidden, the birthday child calls the guests back into the party room. The first guest to spot the hidden toy yells, "Huckle Buckle Beanstalk!" and then it's that guest's turn to hide the toy on the next round. Continue playing for several rounds.

Decorations

Make a list of the characters or Bible heroes associated with your costume theme. Make a party banner using a large disposable tablecloth and decorate it with character names and faces. You may write the names on separate pieces of paper, either by hand or with the computer, and then glue each name onto the tablecloth. If you have a theme-related coloring book, characters or scenes may be colored by the birthday child and then glued onto the banner. Continue the name theme by writing names on the driveway, sidewalk, and walkway in sidewalk chalk. Cover the table with plain white paper and put out cups of crayons. Encourage kids to sign the tablecloth with their character names and decorate it.

Cake

Frost a sheet cake and write the Happy Birthday message in frosting in the center. Around the outside, in a different color frosting, write the names of characters or Bible heroes.

Party Favors

Stickers or other items related to the selected theme
Masks
Markers and notebooks
Coloring books related to the theme
Egg heads
Character ID cards

Taste of Italy Party

Italian food and Italian fun make this party a sure-fire winner!
Ages: 5 to 8

Invitations

Start with a rectangle of heavy white paper. Glue on a thick stripe of red and a thick stripe of green construction paper to represent the Italian flag. Write, "Lucia's Taste of Italy Birthday Party!" on the front and the party details on the back.

Activities

Pasta People Lay out an assortment of uncooked pasta, glue, markers, wiggly eyes and pipe cleaners and let the kids create pasta people. Make a few samples before the party to give them ideas. You may spray paint the uncooked pasta before the party to make the pasta people more colorful.

Modified Bocce Have the birthday child roll a large ball (you can use a softball or baseball) into the bocce court (an area that's up to 20' long and 5' wide). Give each guest a smaller ball (you can use golf balls labeled with initials) to roll as close as possible to the large ball without hitting it. The guest with the closest ball wins a small prize, such as a sticker or a stamp on his hand. Play several rounds.

Pizza, Pizza, Spaghetti Play like Duck, Duck, Goose, but substitute names of Italian food.

Pasta Hunt Before the party, gather several kinds of pasta, so there's a different shape for each guest. Put one of each shape of pasta in a bowl and hide at least five others of each shape in the party room or yard. At the party, have the kids draw a pasta shape out of the bowl and then go searching for three more matching shapes. Once they have their four matching pasta shapes, they can trade them in for a prize.

Pasta Architecture Split the kids into teams of two or three and provide each team with the same set of building materials. You might include fifteen strands of uncooked spaghetti, a cup of uncooked rotini, ten uncooked bowtie pasta, two empty paper towel rolls, index cards, paper clips, glue, and pipe cleaners. (You may spray paint the pasta and other materials various colors before the party to make the architecture more colorful). Give the teams ten or fifteen minutes to build the tallest structure they can out of the materials provided. Give out awards for "Tallest Pasta Structure," "Most Attractive Pasta Structure," "Most Creative Pasta Structure," "Widest Pasta Structure," "Sturdiest Pasta Structure," "Most Fragile Pasta Structure," and so on.

Leaning Tower of Pisa Kids stand beside each other in a straight line with their feet touching each other. A parent yells directions like, "Lean to the front!," "Lean to the left!," "Lean to the back!," and "Lean to the right!" and kids lean as far as possible in that direction. Guests who stumble while trying to lean are out of the main line and start a second line of stumblers and continue to follow directions. The last guest in the main line wins a special prize.

Italian Piñata Make a Piñata out of a gift bag, cutting out the bottom and loosely taping it back in place. Fill it with candy and small toys and decorate it with red, white, and green streamers. Run a string through the handles and hang it from the ceiling.

Italian Restaurant Prepare a Pasta Bar, with two or three different types of pasta (spaghetti, angel hair, farfalle, ziti, ravioli) and a couple of different sauces (tomato, alfredo, primavera). Seat the partygoers in the dining area and take their orders as a waitress would. Leave them a bill and have them pay with play money.

Decorations

Use red-and-white checkered tablecloths. Hang a map of Italy on the wall and play Italian music or opera music. Decorate with red, white, and green streamers and balloons. Place carafes of red grape juice and plastic goblets on the table.

Cake

Decorate a rectangular sheet cake to look like the Italian flag with red, white, and green frosting.

Party Favors

Wrap the party favors in a piece of red and white checked fabric. Twist it at the top and tie a ribbon around it.
Red, white, and green jelly beans
Trios of pencils—red, white, and green—along with small pads of paper
Flag stickers
Books about Italy
Pasta people

Hawaiian Luau

This party is bright, colorful, and lush—just like the island!
Ages: 5 to 8

Invitations

Create a ticket to Hawaii for an invitation. Cut colored paper into a rectangle, and print "Destination: Hawaii, Celebration: Brooke's 5th Birthday" on the front. Add airplane and fruit stickers and write the party details on the back.

Activities

Hawaiian Birthday Hat Decoration Buy solid-colored birthday hats, and write the name of a guest on each hat in a bright color. Set up a table with Hawaiian stickers or fruit stickers, glitter, glue, and markers, and let kids decorate their hats.

Island Sunglasses Lay out a pair of play sunglasses for each guest, along with items the kids can use to decorate them, such as beads, small stickers, pipe cleaners which can be shaped into flowers or spirals, colorful buttons, and glue. The kids can create their own island sunglasses.

Hawaiian Island Treasure Hunt This is a treasure hunt to find a hidden box of Hawaiian dress-up clothes for the next activity. Before the party, gather five tropical fruits, such as a coconut, a banana, a kiwi, a pineapple, and an orange. Hide them in somewhat obvious spots throughout the house or yard. Also hide a box filled with the dress-up items for the next activity, and toss some candy in the box as well. Create a simple drawing of the hiding place of the dress-up box, then cut the drawing into five puzzle pieces and tuck each piece of the drawing under a different tropical fruit. At the party, the kids hunt for the puzzle pieces, piece them together, and then find the hidden box.

Pass the Hawaiian Dress-Up Bag Before the party, gather several Hawaiian dress-up clothes, such as loud floral shirts, leis, a grass skirt, a straw hat, sunglasses, and beach sandals, and place them in a bag. Try to have at least two items for each guest. The partygoers sit on the floor in a circle and pass the bag while music is played. The guest holding the bag when the music stops must reach into the bag and put on the item he pulls out. Continue playing until the bag is empty.

Freeze Frame While the kids are still dressed up in their Hawaiian outfits, they can play Freeze Frame. Play the music (Hawaiian music if you have it), and have the kids dance. When the music stops, the kids must hold their positions, freezing for as long as they can. The first kid to move becomes the DJ for the next round and then rejoins the group.

Hawaiian Fruit Relay Race Split the partygoers into two teams. Give each team three or four fruits, such as a banana, an orange, a pineapple, and a coconut. Place the fruits in a basket in front of each team. At "Go!" the first player on each team reaches into the basket, picks up a fruit, and passes it through his legs to the next player in line. That player bends down, gets the fruit, and passes it through his legs to the next player in line. Continue passing the fruit down the line until it has reached the last player in line. That player then runs to the front of the line, gets a new fruit, and passes it through his legs down the line. The first team to pass all the fruits down its line wins. An alternate version of this relay race has guests passing fruit from neck to neck. At parties for younger children, modify this game to be a simple relay race.

Hawaiian Taste Test Get jelly beans in flavors of tropical fruits, such as pineapple, coconut, kiwi, orange, banana, and grapefruit. Have kids sit in a circle and close their eyes. Put one jelly bean in each child's hand. Once everyone has one, they can taste it. Let the kids yell out their guesses and award a pineapple sticker for each correct guess. The guest with the most number of pineapple stickers at the end of the game wins a special prize.

Hawaiian Piñata Cut the bottom out of a colorful gift bag, and then loosely tape it back in place. Place candy, favors, and red, orange, and yellow confetti in the bag, and decorate it with orange, red, and yellow ribbon and streamers. Run string through the handles and hang it in the party room or yard.

Hawaiian Sundae Set up a table with sundae ingredients including pineapple topping, strawberry topping, hot fudge, candies, crushed cookies, banana slices, cherries, and ice cream. Let the guests make their own tropical fruit sundaes.

Decorations

Outside, tie a bunch of pink, yellow, red, and orange balloons to the mailbox or lamppost. Stick Tiki torches in the ground. Write "Aloha" in sidewalk chalk on the driveway or on a sign. Add beach balls, seashells, beach chairs, beach pails, and beach umbrellas. Place the watermelon boat (described below) on the party table.

Cake

Serve a Hawaiian cake by making a rectangular sheet cake and decorating it with a palm tree statue and Hawaiian figurines. For drinks, serve fruit slushes made by mixing a can of frozen fruit punch, one can of water, and some ice in a blender. For added fun, serve the slushes in coconut cups. Also serve fruit ka-bobs in a carved out boat of watermelon.

Party Favors

Sunglasses
Leis
Kiwi fruit
Fruit stickers
Fruit flavored candy
Coconut cups

Outer Space Party

Captivate your child's active imagination with this creative party.
It can be customized to reflect the latest space movie or characters.
Ages: 5 to 9

Invitations

Cut small paper plates in half and then paint them with silver metallic spray paint. Use a black permanent marker to define windows and a door on the space ship. Write, "Greetings, earthling! Zip on over to Nicholas's house for an out-of-this-world Space Adventure Birthday Party!" on the front of the spaceship and the party details on the back.

Activities

Transformer Decorating Before the party, make transformers for the kids by spray painting one small box (a small jewelry box, a juice box, or an animal cracker box) for each guest in metallic silver paint. Wrap gold or silver play keys or play coins in colorful tissue paper and insert one in each box. At the party, lay out stickers, craft jewels, glue sticks, and markers for the guests to decorate the transformer boxes as they arrive. Once all the guests have arrived, ask them to unwrap the key or coin inside their box. For the remaining activities, those with the gold keys or coins are Space Travelers and those with the silver keys or coins are Aliens.

Dress Up The Space Travelers can dress in futuristic clothes, such as turtlenecks with spaceship logo stickers, Dr. Spock ears, sunglasses, a cord around their neck for the key to their spaceship, and space rings. The aliens can dress in bright, colorful, metallic clothing and face paint (try painting on a third eye or a green face). Take instant photos and give these out as a party favor.

Relay Race to Save Humanity Explain to the kids that the Space Travelers have encountered Aliens in another galaxy and have discovered that they are planning to buy a spaceship and invade earth. To save humanity, the Space Travelers must take all of the Aliens' gold. At the same time, the Aliens are trying to get more money to buy the spaceship, so they are trying to remove all the gold from the Space Travelers' spaceship. Establish a starting line for the relay race, and place one chair at least fifteen or twenty feet away (if the party's outdoors, the chairs can be even further apart). Place a pile of chocolate gold coins on the chair. The first guest on each team must run to the chair, pick up a gold coin, put it in his transformer box, and run back to line with it. When he gets back to the starting line, the next guest in line runs to the chair, picks up a gold coin, places it in his transformer box, and runs back to line. The first team to get gold coins in all their transformer boxes wins special prizes.

Close Encounters This active game is ideal to play across a driveway. The Aliens stand on one side of the driveway, and the Space Travelers stand on the other side. The birthday child is "it" in the first round and stands in the center of the driveway. When "it" calls "Run!" the children on both sides of the driveway run to the other side of the driveway while "it" tries to tag them. Anyone who gets tagged joins "it" in the center of the driveway for the next round and helps "it" tag the other children. Keep playing until there's only one runner left. That player becomes "it" in the next round.

Alien Socks Have each guest remove one sock, roll it into a ball, and place it on an open sheet in the middle of the party room or yard. The partygoers stand around the sheet, lift it and hold it about waist-high. The kids lift the sheet up and down together, trying to knock an alien sock onto the ground. The guest whose sock remains on the sheet the longest wins.

Space Mission At the end of this treasure hunt, the Aliens and the Space Travelers will mix together their two bowls of slime ingredients to create space slime. Before the party, mix together 2 cups of white glue, 1 ½ cups warm water, and food coloring. Place this mixture in a covered bowl, label it "Alien Ingredients," and hide the bowl. In a separate bowl, mix together and dissolve 1 ⅓ cups warm water and 1 tablespoon of borax. Label this bowl "Space Traveler Ingredients." Cover it and hide it. Create two series of clues, each leading to a different bowl. Put each set of clues on a different color of paper. At the party, the Aliens and the Space Travelers each follow their clues to try to find the slime ingredients. At the end, the brave ones mix the two bowls of slime ingredients together with their hands to create space slime. Give each guest a resealable plastic bag of space slime to take home.

Spaceship Building Split the guests into teams of three or four. Give each team a set of boxes of various sizes (shoe boxes, cereal boxes, small jewelry-size boxes), silver-painted toilet paper rolls and paper towel rolls, nuts and bolts, springs, pipe cleaners, straws, buttons, tin foil, glue, and other supplies. Give them a fixed amount of time to build a spaceship or a robot.

Outer Space Piñata Make a space piñata out of a silvery gift bag. Cut out the bottom and loosely tape it back in place. Fill the bag with candy, small toys, and metallic confetti. Hang it from the ceiling or a tree by a string run through the handles. Decorate it with streamers, balloons, and hanging spaceship shapes cut from poster board.

Decorations

Decorate with silver Mylar balloons. Use tin foil as a tablecloth and use silvery paper plates, napkins, and cups. Wrap a chair in tin foil for the birthday child's throne. Hang Christmas lights in the party room and create flying saucers to hang from the ceiling by wrapping paper plates in tin foil and attaching string.

Cake

Decorate a sheet cake with nighttime stars, a moon, and planets, and place a small spaceship figurine on top of the cake. Serve with "alien juice," either Orbitz soda or juice with blue food coloring.

Party Favors

Outer space coloring books
Silver pens
Space stickers
Candy
Plastic space rings
Miniature spaceships
Gold coins
Glow-in-the-dark items
Transformer boxes
Space slime

Rainbow Party

This enchanting rainbow party is a festive and active celebration for a colorful birthday!
Ages: 5 to 9

Invitations

The birthday child can use paint or thick markers to create a rainbow on rectangles of heavyweight paper. Fold the rectangles in half and write, "Come to Alexis's Rainbow Birthday Party!" along the curve of the rainbow and write the party details inside. Write, "Be a color!" at the bottom of the invitation, and ask guests to dress in a solid color for the human rainbow. Decorate the envelope with rainbow stickers.

Activities

Rainbow Tie Dye Give each guest one or two 12" square pieces of white fabric, a clothespin, and elastics. Guests can create spiral designs by using clothespins to pinch the center of the fabric, winding it into a flat disk shape, and tightly wrapping elastics around it. Or they may roll the fabric and tightly wrap a few elastics around the roll. Prepare a few different colors of fabric dye according to the directions on the box. The guests dip their fabric into buckets or bowls of the die, rinse, and repeat with another color on another section of the fabric. When the dyeing is complete, guests wash their fabric in a bucket of warm sudsy water, rinse it in cold water, and hang it up to dry.

Rainbow's End Create a pot of gold by filling a glass bowl with chocolate coins wrapped in gold foil. Ask each guest to guess how many coins are in the pot of gold. The guest who comes closest wins a handful of chocolate coins, and everyone else gets one coin as a consolation prize.

Rainbow Bracelets Lay out cording and beads and let the guests create friendship bracelets.

Rainbow Ribbon Before the party, gather several different colors of ribbon or yarn, and attach a wrapped party favor to the end of each one. String the many colors of ribbon throughout the party room or the house (i.e. around the banister, up the stairs, around a doorknob, around a couch, under a table, etc.). Give each guest a clothespin and the end of one strand of ribbon. Let them wrap the ribbon around the clothespin as they follow the trail to the "pot of gold" at the end of their rainbow.

Rainbow Race Arrange chairs in a circle facing outward, so there's one fewer chairs than guests. Put the names of colors into a hat and let each guest draw a color out of the hat. The kids memorize their color and then return their slip of paper to the hat and sit down. The birthday child is "it" and does not sit down. He draws a name of a color out the hat, yells it out, and the guest with that color has to get up and run around the circle of chairs and try to sit back in his chair again. At the same time, the child who is "it" tries to sit in the vacated chair. Whoever is left without a chair is "it" for the next round and draws the name of another color. Continue playing several rounds.

Rainbow Relay Split the guests into two teams and give each team a box or container filled with markers of several different colors, so there's one marker for each guest. Post a blank piece of paper at the finish line and have the teams stand behind the starting line. At "Go!" the first child in each team runs to the paper, selects a marker, draws an arc, and runs back to the line. She hands the box of markers to the next guest, who runs to the paper, selects a different marker, draws and arc over the first one, and runs back to line. The guests continue until a rainbow has been drawn using every color in the box without repeating one. If a color is repeated, the team must start over. The first team to complete their rainbow wins.

Create a Rainbow Practice this before the party. You'll need a bright, sunny day. With your back to the sun, spray a fine mist from a hose or sprinkler in front of you against a dark background. A rainbow should appear in the stream of water. Let the kids take turns holding the hose. This works best in the early morning or late afternoon.

Rainbow Scavenger Hunt In this outdoor scavenger hunt, the teams race against each other to find an object in every color on their list. Split the partygoers into teams of three or four guests. Give each team a bag and the same list of colors—although for pre-readers the colors may be drawn on the list with markers rather than spelled out. Specify the boundaries and a time limit, and instruct the teams to find one object for each color on the list and place it in their bag. Objects must be small enough to fit in the bag. At parties for older kids, you can request varying numbers of items for each color, such as six different green items, two different pink items, four different red items, and so on. If the weather is inclement, this scavenger hunt can be played indoors by giving each team a few magazines and pairs of scissors.

Rainbow Price Is Right (ages 7 and up) Gather several party favors, one for each color of the rainbow. Write the price of each favor on a slip of paper and place the price facedown behind the favor. Give each guest a piece of paper and pencil. One by one, hold up each favor, describe it, and ask guests to write down their guess of the price. The child with the guess that's closest to the actual price (without going over the actual price) wins the party favor.

Human Rainbow The guests line up according to the colors they're wearing to create a human rainbow. If you have an instant camera, take photos and hand them out as party favors. Otherwise send a photo of the human rainbow out with thank you cards.

Decorations

This is a great opportunity to use all your leftover paper goods from past birthday parties, because each place setting at the party table can be set with a different color paper cup, paper plate, and napkin. Put down a paper tablecloth. Draw a big rainbow in the center and put cups of crayons and markers on the party table for the guests to add more rainbows to the tablecloth. Toss some colorful confetti in the center of the party table, and decorate with multi-colored balloons and streamers. Hang rainbow artwork around the party room, and use sidewalk chalk to draw rainbows on the driveway.

Cake

Divide the cake batter into four bowls and add a different color of food coloring to each bowl. Pour the colors into the baking pans one at a time to create layers of color. Frost the cake with a colorful rainbow made from icing. Serve lukewarm clear soda in clear cups along with colored ice cubes, which are made by adding food coloring to the water in your ice cube trays.

Party Favors

Kaleidoscopes
Colorful crazy straws
Rainbow stickers
Rainbow pencils
Rainbow notebooks
Rainbow tie-dyed cloths

Mad Scientist Party

Fascinate, amaze, and entertain your guests with these demonstrations and games!
Ages: 5 to 10

Invitations

Fold a rectangle of colored paper in half and cut paper of a different color into the shape of a fluted beaker. Glue the beaker onto the cover of the invitation and draw in bubbles just above the beaker. Write "You're Invited to Anthony's Mad Scientist Birthday Party!" on the front cover and write the party details inside.

Activities

Microscope Quiz If you have, or can borrow a microscope, make up a few slides of household items and let the kids try to guess what they're looking at under the microscope while you're waiting for all the guests to arrive.

Mad Scientist Party

Hunt for the Secret Jelly Beans Before the party, get several different flavors of jelly beans and place a handful of each flavor into an empty film canister. Fill each canister with a different flavor, making sure there are enough in each canister for every guest to have one. Hide the canisters throughout the party room or yard and create a treasure hunt leading the guests from one canister to the next. Tuck a clue under each canister that directs the kids to the next one. For pre-readers, the clues can be simple drawings of where to find the next canister. As the kids find the jelly bean canisters, they can turn them over to an adult to be used in the next game. The final canister should be accompanied by a party favor for each guest.

Taste Test Once the guests have completed the treasure hunt, conduct a taste test with the secret jelly beans . Hand out each flavor, one at a time, and let the guests shout out their guess of the jelly bean flavor. At parties for older kids, the guests can write their guesses on a piece of paper. Each flavor will have a different number of points, and a tally at the end will determine the best taster. Once the jelly bean taste test is complete, the guests may progress to a Coke and Pepsi taste test, where the sodas are poured into paper cups of two different colors and guests try to distinguish between the two sodas. Keep a tally to determine the favorite soda. Other taste tests include a potato chip taste test and an ice cream taste test.

Nose Test Find about eight items with pungent smells, such as an orange slice, suntan lotion, a banana, rubbing alcohol, cinnamon, vinegar, a flower, etc. (You can include water to make it more challenging!) Put these items in little paper cups, and cover each one with cheesecloth so that the scent still comes through. Number each sample and make up blank sheets with corresponding numbers for the kids to fill in. At the party, blindfold the kids and wave the samples under their noses, one at a time. Ask them each to write down what they think is in the cup. Give everyone a scratch-n-sniff sticker for participating, and give the child with the most correct guesses a special prize, like a plastic nose. At parties with younger children, the kids can yell out their guesses rather than writing them on a piece of paper.

Magnet Relay Race Split the kids into two teams. Establish a starting line and mark the goal with two chairs. Give each team a large magnet and an empty bowl. Empty a box of paper clips onto each chair. The first child in each line must run to the chair, pick up as many paper clips as he can with the magnet, run back to the line, and put them in the bowl. He hands the magnet to the next guest in line and then goes to the end of the line. Continue until one team has all their paper clips in their bowl.

Kitchen Magic Bring the kids into the kitchen to try these experiments. See if they can predict the results.

Milk Colorbursts The kids squeeze a few different food-color drops into small bowls of hot milk (just a tablespoon or two of milk is needed), then they squeeze a drop of dishwashing detergent in the center of the color. The colors will "burst."

Egg Detective Show the kids two eggs. One has been hard-boiled and the other is raw. Pass the eggs around and ask the kids to guess which is hard-boiled. Then show them the way to tell the difference. Spin the eggs on the floor and then gently touch each one with a finger. One will stop and the other will wobble. The one that wobbles is the raw egg because the yolk causes it to wobble.

Rising Globs The partygoers mix a few tablespoons of colored water with a few tablespoons of vegetable oil, then add salt. The salt will form "globs" that will sink to the bottom and then rise back to the top.

Invisible Ink Show the kids a piece of paper that has a message written in lemon juice (do this before the party by dipping a toothpick or Q-tip in lemon juice and writing with it). The message will appear invisible. Make the message appear by applying a heat source to the paper, such as a flame from a candle, a hot iron, or a hot light bulb. The message can say "Happy Birthday, Jamie!" or it can pose the question in the next Kitchen Magic activity.

Liquid Separation Ask kids to guess which three liquids in your kitchen can be poured into the same clear plastic cup and still remain separate. Try a few of the guesses to see if they work. Then reveal the answer: molasses, oil, and water.

Dry Ice Add warm water to dry ice and watch it steam and billow.

Decorations

Put a "Science Lab" sign in front of your home and attach balloons. Draw chalk footprints leading up the driveway and walkway. Place glass bottles and jars around the party room. Wear a lab coat and plastic gloves.

Cake

Make a science cake by cutting a sheet cake into the shape of a fluted beaker. Place a few gumdrops over the beaker to represent bubbles. Serve root beer floats with the cake. Fill glasses halfway with soda and then have the kids add a scoop of vanilla ice cream and watch their sodas fizz.

Party Favors

Black horn-rim glasses
Magnifying glasses
Magnets
Seeds
Crystals
Rock candy

Parties for Children Ages 6-12

Grandmother's Attic Party

Send guests on an exciting exploration of an old attic filled with mystery, intrigue, and treasures—even if the attic isn't a real one.

Ages: 6 to 9

Invitations

Cut a scrap of small-patterned wallpaper or wrapping paper into the shape of a teacup or teapot. Glue the teacup to the outside of a rectangle of solid-colored paper that's been folded in half. Write, "Come Explore Grandmother's Attic in Celebration of Rachel's 7th Birthday!" around the teacup and write the party details inside.

Activities

Frame Decorating Before the party, buy small mats used for framing. Lay these out on a table along with glue, paintbrushes, and a variety of colored tissue paper that has been cut into one-inch squares. The guests use the paintbrushes to apply the glue to the mat and then lay the tissue paper squares on the glue, folding the tissue paper over the edges of the mat. Once the mat is covered with tissue paper squares, guests may glue decorative touches to the frame such as dried flowers, buttons, confetti, small seashells, or ribbon. Let the frames dry.

Pass the Present Ahead of time, get several keys. Tie a different color ribbon around each key, and hide them in the party room or yard. There should be one for each guest. Create a drawing clue for each hiding place (or, for parties of older children, create challenging word clues). Tuck a clue inside a small party favor for each guest, such as a miniature pad of paper or a change purse. Wrap each party favor individually. Put them all inside a small box and wrap that box. Place the wrapped box inside a slightly larger box, and wrap it. Again, find a slightly larger box, place the wrapped present inside it, and wrap it. Continue adding boxes and wrapping them so that the presents are inside several nested boxes. At the party, the kids sit on the floor in a circle and pass the present from one child to the next while music is played. When the music stops, the guest holding the box unwraps it. If it's another wrapped box, start the music and the box gets passed again. Keep going until the final box is unwrapped, and then each guest selects a favor from the smallest box.

Treasure Hunt This is a hunt to find the hidden key that will unlock the treasure chest filled with the clothes for the dress up activity. The key doesn't need to really work to open the chest. Once the Pass the Present game has ended, instruct the guests to look inside their pads of paper or change purses to find a clue. They should all follow their clues to find their hidden keys. Once all the keys have been found, lead the guests to the treasure chest or chest of drawers, which is covered with sheets and hidden away in the attic room of your house. Remove the sheets to uncover the chest, which has been wrapped with a ribbon. The guest who has the matching ribbon on her key cuts the ribbon and opens the chest. Inside will be a small gift for that guest, as well as party favors and dress up clothes for everyone. (At parties for older children, consider creating a second set of clues leading to the hidden treasure chest.)

Dress Up Fill an old chest or a drawer of a bureau with interesting, retro dress-up clothes, such as shoes, gloves, hats, shawls, purses, boas, scarves, jewelry, and perfume. For boys, include formal clothes such as ties, gloves, jackets, and hats. Put out a full-length mirror. Also set up a nail polish table and help the girls with manicures or nail art. An older sister or a neighborhood teenager may help out with this activity. Older girls may enjoy a makeup station. If boys will be at the party, set up a station for temporary tattoos and face-painting of moustaches, beards, and sideburns. Once the kids are dressed up, take instant photos and tape the photos to the backs of the frames they decorated earlier.

Ha The dressed-up children lie on the floor in a circle, each laying his or her head on the stomach of the next child in the chain. The birthday child begins by saying, "ha." Then the next child in the circle says, "ha ha," and the next says, "ha ha ha." Keep going around the circle, adding a "ha" every time. See who will break the chain by laughing the wrong number of "ha's" on his turn.

Decorations

Decorate the "attic" area of the house with fake cobwebs, furniture draped with sheets, and dim lighting. Set the birthday table formally with a long tablecloth, unlit candlesticks, nice dishes, and a doily at each place setting.

Place the cake on old-fashioned-looking cookie tins. Drape the birthday child's "throne" with a lacey tablecloth.

Cake

Serve tea and crumpets. For the tea, serve lukewarm decaffeinated or herbal flavored teas in teapots and teacups. For crumpets, cut sandwiches into hearts, stars, and other shapes using a cookie cutter or knife. Serve birthday cupcakes topped with small silk flowers.

Party Favors

Decorated picture frames and poster putty for hanging
Instant photos
Keys
Small notebooks or change purses
Silk flowers from the cupcakes
Perfume
Sachets

Architect Party

Kids who love to build and create will enjoy the challenging games at this party.
Ages: 6 to 10

Invitations

Fold a piece of paper in half. Cut it into the shape of a house. Cut out holes for windows on the front cover and tape a clear plastic sheet inside the front cover for glass windows. Write the words "Mason's Architect Birthday Party" on the inside so they can be seen through the windows. Write the party details inside.

Activities

Pretzel Log Cabins Give each guest a small, clean milk carton and set out peanut butter and small stick pretzels in bowls. Let the guests each construct a pretzel log cabin by attaching the pretzels to the milk carton using the peanut butter. Use a few different sizes of pretzels.

Architect Party

Architectural Drawing Give each guest a piece of graph paper, a pencil, and some drawing tools. Ask them to use their imaginations to draw their dream houses. When the drawings are complete, sit on the floor in a circle and ask kids to briefly explain their drawings to each other.

Building Contest The object of this game is to build the tallest building using household items. The teams are selected by having each guest draw a coin from a bowl (pennies, nickels, and dimes) to determine which team he's on. Each team gets the same set of starting materials, such as building blocks, empty tissue boxes, toilet paper rolls, paper towel rolls, pipe cleaners, straws, empty bottles, bottle caps, buttons, glue, string, pencils, paper clips, index cards, toothpicks, uncooked spaghetti, etc. (Some of the items can be spray painted before the party to make the structures more colorful.) Set the timer. The team with the tallest building when the timer sounds wins all the coins. Give consolation prizes for most attractive, most colorful, etc.

House Treasure Hunt Before the party, place a small party favor into a house, a small storage box such as a diaper wipe box or an index card box. There should be one house and one party favor for each guest. Tie ribbons around the boxes and attach labels to the ribbon. Give each box a unique address and write the address on the label. Hide the boxes in an area of the house or yard, and create a large map with the addresses on it. Roll up the map and place it in an empty wrapping paper roll. Write each address on a piece of paper, insert it into a balloon, and blow up the balloon. At the party, let each child select a balloon, pop it, read the address of his or her treasure house, get the map out of its case, refer to the map to find the location of his house, and then find his house. Each guest brings the house to a parent who verifies that the addresses match and then cuts the ribbon so the guest can get his party favor inside. (Variation: if kids are too young to read addresses, then use house colors instead of addresses.)

House Relay Race Split the kids into two teams. Establish a starting line and put four chairs at the finish line. On two of the chairs, build a house using building blocks. The first guest in each team must run to a chair with blocks and move the house to an empty chair by disassembling it and rebuilding it, and then run back to the line. When he slaps the hand of the next team member, that guest runs to the chairs, takes the house down, and rebuilds it back on the first chair. He then runs back, and so on, alternating chairs with each turn. The first team to finish wins a special prize.

Decorations

Decorate the party room with large architectural blueprints if you can get them. They would also make a great tablecloth. Also decorate the table with drafting supplies and construction materials.

Cake

Cut a sheet cake in the shape of a tall, thin building and decorate it with candy windows and doors.

Party Favors

Drafting supplies such as mini-scissors, compasses, protractors, tracing shapes
Building puzzles
Plastic pouches
Mini locks and keys
House stickers

Chinatown Party

Take-out food, chopsticks, customized fortune cookies,
and great games make this party a big hit!

Ages: 6 to 10

Invitations

Use Chinese take-out boxes to hold the party invitations. Write the invited guest's name on the outside of the box using a permanent marker and place the invitation inside. Write the party details on a piece of red paper or use a computer to print the invitations on red paper. Then roll the red paper up scroll-style, tie it with a ribbon, and drop it in the takeout box on a bed of red and black confetti. Hand deliver these invitations.

Activities

China Place Mats Before the party, photocopy a map of China onto white paper. At the party, set these maps out on a table along with glitter glue, stickers, crayons, and markers. The kids can color and decorate their maps of China. Cover the maps with clear contact paper and use the place mats later in the party.

Orient Express Relay Race Label shoeboxes with the names of cities in China, such as Beijing, Hong Kong, Shanghai, Chengdu, and Canton. Place a few chocolate gold coins in each box and scatter the boxes around the party room or yard. At the party, split the kids into two teams and establish a starting line. Each team gets a pair of chopsticks and an empty bowl for their coins. The first child in line runs to any box, picks up a gold coin with his chopsticks, carries it back to the starting line, and deposits the coin in the team's bowl. If the coin is dropped, the guest must leave it on the ground and go back to get another one. The first runner then passes the chopsticks to the next child in line, who runs to any box, picks up a gold coin with her chopsticks, brings it back, deposits it in the team's bowl, and hands the chopsticks to the next child in line. Place a different number of coins in each box so that some boxes will run out of gold coins before others, and kids will have to hunt around to find a box with coins. The first team to get fifteen coins in their bowl keeps all the gold coins, splitting them among the teammates. To make this game more challenging for older kids, write a point value on each gold coin with a permanent marker and give a special award to the team with the highest number of points at the end of the race.

Chinese Fortune Hunt Before the party, buy some fortune cookies and customize the fortune inside the cookie by removing the fortunes with tweezers and inserting your own. Each customized fortune will contain a clue of where a party favor is hidden, as well as a number. For pre-readers, the clue may be a hand-drawn picture of the hiding spot of the party favor. Hide the party favors, and number each one to correspond with the number on the clue. Kids can open the fortune cookies and then hunt for their party favor. They must confirm it's theirs by matching the two numbers.

Huckle Buckle China Get a miniature panda bear (or other object that reminds you of China) and show it to all the kids. The birthday child then hides the panda bear somewhere in the designated room while the guests wait in another room. The hidden panda bear must be visible without moving anything in the room. The waiting kids are called in once the panda bear is hidden, and with their hands behind their backs, they walk around the room looking for the hidden panda bear. As soon as a guest spots it, he yells "Huckle Buckle China!" Then that guest hides the panda bear while the others wait in another room, and another round of the game is played. Play several rounds.

Piñata Cut the bottom out of a red shopping bag or gift bag, and then loosely tape it back in place. Place candy, favors, and red confetti in the bag, and decorate it with red and black ribbon and streamers. Run string through the handles and hang it in the party room or yard.

Dinner at Chinatown The guests can take off their shoes, sit on the floor, and eat from a low dinner table. Put out chopsticks and teacups and serve Chinese take-out food.

Decorations

Tie black and red helium balloons to your mailbox or lamppost outside and write "This way to Chinatown" in sidewalk chalk on your driveway. Use Christmas lights and red and black streamers, ribbons, and balloons to decorate the party room. Set the party table with red and black plates, napkins, and cups. Scatter large pillows on the floor, and place several take-out containers stuffed with red and black tissue paper around the party room. Use the China map place mats at the party table.

Cake

Serve individual cupcakes, each decorated with a miniature fan or a miniature Chinese umbrella.

Party Favors

Place the party favors in Chinese food containers. Tie a balloon to each container for guests to take home.

Customized fortune cookies ("Thanks for coming to my party! Amy")

Chopsticks personalized with the party guest's name using a permanent marker or puff paint

Miniature fans

Miniature panda bears

Small paper dragons

Glamour Girl Party

*This party is a real treat for girls who show an interest
in glamour, beauty, and primping.*
Ages: 6 to 12

Invitations

Buy a package of inexpensive foam curlers at a drugstore or discount store. Cut colorful paper into narrow strips to create invitations that are no wider than the curlers. Wrap the invitation around the foam curler as if it were a strand of hair. Place it inside an envelope and hand deliver.

Activities

Face Collage Before the party, cut out several large photos of faces from magazines and glue each photo to a piece of heavyweight paper. Lay these photos out on a table along with glue and an assortment of dried beans (including kidney beans, lentils, green peas, lima beans, navy beans, chick peas), peas, and popping corn. Place each type of bean in a small paper cup or in the cup of a muffin tin. At the party, as the guests arrive, they create a face collage by covering a photo with a variety of beans and gluing them on. For example, one guest may decide to use kidney beans for the hair, lima beans for the eyes, navy beans for the eyebrows, and corn for the teeth. Create a sample collage before the party for the guests to follow.

Barrette Decorating Set up a table with barrettes, puff paints, ribbon rosettes, miniature dice, spray-painted puzzle pieces, charms, beads, and glue, and let the guests decorate barrettes.

Safety Pin Beading Lay out several different sizes of safety pins and a variety of beads and charms. Guests string the beads onto the safety pins, then hang a few beaded safety pins off of a larger one. They can pin them to their shirts, shoelaces, backpacks, or hats.

Friendship Bracelets Lay out a few different colors of cording and some beads and let the guests create friendship bracelets.

Beauty Makeovers Once everyone has arrived at the party, take them on a journey to your beauty parlor, which is a room in your home that you have transformed with blow dryers, makeup, brushes, beauty supplies, hair accessories, and magazine photos up on the walls. Set up several beauty stations, such as a station for manicures or nail art, a station for pedicures, a station for facials, a station for makeup (if the girls are old enough), a station for hair beading, a station for hair styling, and a station for scalp massages. Hire a few high school girls or ask some friends to help out as beauticians. Let the guests rotate among the stations to receive their beauty makeovers.

Glamour Girl Party

Photo Shoot Using an instant camera (or a regular camera, if you have a nearby one-hour photo developing place), take photos of each girl, insert them into a frame, and give them out as party favors. Make sure you also take a group photo. After the party, create a photo album for the birthday girl.

Dress-Up Relay Race Put an outfit consisting of a hat, necklace, dress, and shoes in a suitcase. Split the guests into two teams. Establish a starting line and place the suitcase on a chair at least 15' or 20' from the starting line. The first guest in each line must run to the suitcase, put on the entire outfit, and run back to the line. The other guests must then help her remove the outfit and dress the next child in line, who must then run around the chair and back, and so on. The last guest must undress, put the outfit back into the suitcase, and put the suitcase back on the chair. The first team with the suitcase back on the chair wins a special prize. If you have a video camera, tape this game and play it back for the kids while they eat their cake.

Glamour Girl Memory Gather about fifteen glamour objects, such as lipstick, a brush, and nail polish. Put the objects on a large tray, and cover it with a cloth. The girls sit in a circle on the floor, and each one receives a piece of paper and a pencil. (They may work in pairs if not all are proficient writers.) Put the tray on the floor and remove the cloth for about thirty seconds. Ask the kids to look carefully at everything on the tray. Then remove the tray and give them five minutes to write down from memory as many objects as they can remember. The child or the pair that remembers the highest number of objects wins a prize.

Glamour Girl Price Is Right (ages 7 and up) Use the glamour objects from the previous game and line these up across a table. Write the price of each item on a slip of paper and place the price facedown behind the item. Give each guest a piece of paper and pencil. One by one, hold up each item, describe it, and ask guests to write down their guess of the price. The partygoer with the guess that's closest to the actual price (without going over the actual price) wins the item.

Cake

After their makeovers, take the girls out for pizza so they can show off their new looks. Serve cupcakes decorated with licorice and candies to look like little faces for dessert. Open gifts at the pizza parlor.

Party Favors

Magazines
Hair combs, clips, or other hair accessories
Hair beads
Nail polish
Photos
Frames for photos
Lip-gloss
Cologne
Cosmetic cases

Apple Orchard Party

This fun party begins with guests each baking an individual apple pie!
Ages: 6 to 12

Invitations

Cut red or green poster board into apple shapes and write the party details on them. Cut each apple into several puzzle pieces and mail. The recipient must piece the puzzle together to read the invitation.

Activities

Apple Bag Decorating Give each child a sturdy, white paper bag. Set out stickers, markers, glitter, and glue sticks and let the kids decorate their apple bags. You can also give the kids canvas bags or burlap bags to decorate with fabric paint and iron-on cutout letters and shapes.

Apple Pie Baking Make the pie crust dough ahead of time, and have the kids roll it out and place it in individual-sized pie tins. Have some peeled and sliced apples ready for the kids to mix with sugar and cinnamon. Then have them place the apples in the piecrusts. Bake the pies while the other activities take place.

Apple People Set up a table with peeled apples, butter knives, spoons, jars, miniature marbles, cotton, pencils, uncooked popcorn kernels, dried peas, straight pins, etc. Give the guests peeled apples, and have them carve the face of a person into the apple using butter knives. They can carve deep holes for the eyes, and then insert the miniature marbles or dried peas inside for eyeballs. For the nose, they can carve recesses around the nose area to give it definition, then carve out nostrils. And they can carve an open mouth and fill it with corn kernels for teeth. Pin cotton to the top of the head for hair. Stick a pencil into the bottom of the apple, and stand it up by putting the pencil in a jar or small bottle. You may need to put some rocks or sand in the bottom of the jar to weigh it down. The apple should be in open air above the jar, not touching or leaning against anything. By the end of the party, these apple people will start to turn brown. In the days after the party, they'll continue their transformation by becoming shriveled, wrinkled, and scary-looking!

Apple Picking If you're lucky enough to have a real apple orchard nearby, take the kids to the orchard, give them each a basket, and pick apples. Hayrides may also be available at the apple orchard.

Apple Orchard Treasure Hunt This is a good replacement for picking real apples if you don't have an orchard nearby. Get small party favors for the guests. Place half of them in one box and half in another. Wrap the boxes and hide them in two different locations. Develop two series of clues leading from one location to the next, with one set of clues written on green construction paper and the other on red. The last clue should lead the guests to the hidden box of favors. For pre-readers, use instant photos or drawings of the hiding spots of the clues. To assign teams, place an assortment of red and green apples in a deep bowl or bucket. Each guest draws an apple from the bucket to determine which team he's on—the red team or the green team. Each team follows the clues sequentially to find their hidden present.

Apple Cup Contest Buy a few packages of small, bathroom paper cups (in red or with an apple design if you can find them). Split the guests into a few teams so that there are about three or four guests per team. Give each team a package of paper cups and plenty of floor space. The teams race against the clock to build the highest structure they can with the paper cups. Set a defined time limit, such as five or ten minutes.

Cake

Serve warm apple pie a la mode.

Party Favors

Individual apple pies
Apple bags
Apples that each guest picked
Red or green apples from treasure hunt
Apple people
Caramel apples
Apple stickers
Pencils with apple-shaped erasers
Apple flavored jelly beans
Apple flavored lip-gloss or Chapstick

Pop Star Party

Kids enjoy playing the role of their favorite pop star at this party!
Ages: 7 to 12

Invitations

Make CD invitations by cutting poster board into circles, punching holes in the centers, and spray painting each circle with metallic silver paint. Write the party details on the front of the disc in block lettering as you would see on a CD. If the invitations will be hand delivered, you can enclose each one in its own plastic CD case. Include instructions: "We'll be putting on a rock concert. Bring a CD with your favorite song and be ready to lip-synch it, either alone or with a group."

Activities

Hollywood Boulevard Before the party, draw several stars on the driveway using sidewalk chalk and write each guest's name in a star. As guests arrive, they can trace their feet right next to their star.

Pop Star Party

Autograph Books Buy small notebooks as a party favor. Write a heading on each of the first few pages of the books, such as, "Autographs," "Favorite Pop Star," "Favorite Song," "Favorite Pizza," "Favorite Color," "Favorite Movie," and "Favorite Movie Star." Let the guests decorate the covers on their books with stickers, markers, and glitter glue. Then let them ask other guests to autograph their books and fill in some of their personal favorites on each page.

Pop Star Sunglasses Pop stars need to be incognito, so each one of the guests needs a good pair of sunglasses. Set out a table with inexpensive children's sunglasses, glue, feathers, glitter, small plastic objects, and beads, and let the kids make a statement by decorating their own sunglasses.

Pop Star Dress-Up Pay a visit to the thrift shop and pick up wild clothes that a pop star might wear. Add clothes from your own family collection, including lots of brightly colored clothes, black items, and any clothes with animal prints. Put these out along with wigs of long hair, glitter spray for hair, black nail polish, face paint, eyeliner, temporary tattoos, boots, and earrings. The kids dress up as pop stars. If you have any musical instruments or microphones on hand, they are fun props. Take an instant photo of each guest.

Rock Concert Give each guest the opportunity to perform, either in a group or solo act, but don't force anyone who's resistant. Designate a stage area. Hang a black cloth backdrop with silver foil stars attached to it, and set up chairs for the other kids to sit in to watch the performances. Give the performers microphones, play the song they designate, and let the kids lip-synch it. If you have any guitars or other musical instruments, let kids use these as props. If you have a video camera, videotape the acts. Play the videotape back later in the party. Consider karaoke as an alternative to lip-synching if you have a karaoke system or know someone who does.

Music Awards Create or buy several awards and make sure that each performer or performing group wins one. Awards may include "Best Group," "Best Dancing," "Best Female Performer," "Best Male Performer," "Most Realistic Performance," "Best Lip-Synching," and "Best Overall."

Pop Star Groupie Arrange chairs in a circle facing outward, so there's one fewer chair than guests. Put the names of famous pop stars into a hat and let each guest draw a name out of the hat. The kids memorize their pop star's name and then return their slip of paper to the hat and sit down. The birthday child is the groupie and does not sit down. He draws a name of a pop star out of the hat and yells it out. That guest has to get up and run around the circle of chairs and try to sit back in his chair again. At the same time, the groupie tries to sit in the vacated chair. Whoever's left without a chair is the groupie for the next round and draws the name of another pop star. Continue playing several rounds.

Freeze Frame One guest (the first time, it can be the birthday child) is the DJ. The remaining guests all dance to rock and roll music using wild and exaggerated movements. The DJ stops the music, and all the kids must freeze their positions. The first guest to move is out and then becomes the DJ for the next round.

Decorations

Hang CDs from the ceiling with ribbon. Decorate with black and white balloons, streamers, and cutouts of musical notes and guitars. Post a sign in front of your house, "Rock Concert Here Today." Using sidewalk chalk, write, "Hollywood Boulevard" on the driveway and draw big stars.

Cake

Bake a round cake, cut a hole out of the center of it, and decorate it to look like a CD.

Party Favors

Sunglasses
Autograph books
Water bottles
Pencils or pens with guitar design
Guitar key chains

Chocolate Party

*For the chocolate fanatic, this celebration of candy making
and sophisticated games is sure to delight!*
Ages: 7 to 12

Invitations

Buy candy bars with double wrappers, such as Kit Kat bars. Remove the
outer wrapper and replace it with a homemade wrapper that is actually the
party invitation. Use colored paper and in large block lettering on the front
of the candy bar, print, "Jenna's Chocolate Birthday Party", and then include
the party details on the back of the wrapper. Cut the wrapper to size and use
a glue stick to hold it in place.

Activities

Candy Factory Buy multi-colored candy tablets, candy molds, lollipop
molds, paintbrushes, and lollipop sticks from a party goods store or a specialty

store. Melt the candy and help the kids make candies to bring home as a party favor. Older kids can make multi-colored candies using the paintbrushes, and the younger children can make lollipops.

Guessing Game Have the guests guess how many chocolate malt balls or M&Ms are in a glass jar. The child with the closest guess keeps the candy jar.

Pass the Present Get assorted candy bars, a different one for each guest. Place these in a small box and wrap the box. Then put this wrapped box inside a slightly bigger box, and wrap it. Put the wrapped boxes inside another slightly bigger box, and wrap it. Keep adding boxes and wrapping until you have one wrapped large present with nested boxes inside. At the party, play music as the kids sit on the floor in a circle and pass the present from one child to the next. When the music stops, the guest holding the box can open it. If it's another wrapped box, start the music and the box gets passed again. Keep going until the final box is opened, then each child gets a chocolate bar from the smallest box. The child who opened the final box selects the first candy bar, then the box is passed around the circle for each guest to select a bar. The chocolate bar selected by each guest in this activity will be important for the following Chocolate Treasure Hunt and the Chocolate Chairs game.

Chocolate Treasure Hunt Before the party, write the name of each candy bar in the Pass the Present activity on a tag. Tie the tags to party favors and hide them in various spots throughout the party room or yard. Write a clue for each hiding place on the back of an index card, and write the name of a candy bar on the front. If the kids are pre-readers, then the clue can be a drawing of the location of the hidden party favor. At the party, lay the index card clues on a table and let the kids find the clue that corresponds with the candy bar they selected in the Pass the Present activity. Once all the guests have their clues, the hunt for the party favors can begin!

Chocolate Relay Race Split the kids into two teams and ask the teams to line up. Give each team a paper cup and twenty-five Tootsie Rolls in a bag. Place the Tootsie Roll bag at the front of the line, and place an empty bowl at the end of the line. The object of the race is to transfer all the Tootsie Rolls from the bag to the bowl, one at a time. The first guest in line picks up a Tootsie Roll from the bag, places it in the cup, and passes the cup to the next guest in line. The kids pass the cup down the line until it reaches the end, and that guest drops the Tootsie Roll into the bowl. Then he runs to the front of the line and picks up a new Tootsie Roll and places it in the cup, and remains at the front of the line. He then passes the cup to the next guest, and it continues down the line to the end, where the last person in line drops the Tootsie Roll in the bowl and then runs to the front of the line, gets a new Tootsie Roll, and so on. The sequence of the line will continually change throughout this activity, and the guests may need coaching depending on their age. The first team to fill the bowl with the twenty-five Tootsie Rolls wins. At parties for younger children, you can modify this activity to be a traditional relay race.

Chocolate Chairs You'll need the index cards with the candy bar names and a circle of chairs facing outward. There should be one chair less than the number of guests. The guests sit in the chairs, and the birthday child stands on the side and pulls an index card out of a bowl. He then yells the name of that chocolate bar. The guest with that chocolate bar must get up from his chair, run in a circle, and get back to the chair, while the birthday child tries to get to the chair first. Whoever is left without a seat is "it" for the next round. Play several rounds.

Chocolate Fondue Before the party, cut bananas, strawberries, cantaloupe, pineapple, grapes, pound cake, and angel food cake into cubes. At the party, add one-half cup of heavy cream to a bag of chocolate chips and melt the mixture over a double boiler. If you have a fondue pot, keep the melted chocolate warm with a low flame. Let the kids spear the fruit with wooden sticks, dip it into the melted chocolate mixture, and eat it.

Decorations

Use the color silver for the decorations and keep them simple, sophisticated, and delicious. Start with a silver foil tablecloth scattered with M&Ms and Hershey's kisses. Add silver plates, cups, and balloons. Create a silver throne for the birthday child by covering a chair with tin foil and attaching candy bar wrappers.

Cake

Make or buy an ice cream cake. Decorate it with strands of melted chocolate. Serve along with the chocolate fondue.

Party Favors

Place the party favors in small, white, candy boxes that are often sold with candy making supplies.
Homemade candies
Recipe cards for chocolate fondue
Stickers of chocolates
Small memo pads of paper with chocolate designs

Parties for Pre-Teens

Camping Party

The older set will enjoy the independence of this fun sleepover
celebration that can be held outdoors in a real tent or inside.
Ages: 8 to 12

Invitations

Create an invitation that looks like a person in a sleeping bag. Fold a square of heavyweight paper in half, then cut a few inches off the top of the front cover. Draw a person's face on the top of the inside right page, and decorate the front cover to look like a sleeping bag with a zipper using silver glitter glue. Write "Camping Party!" on the outside, and the party details inside.

Activities

Tent Set-Up The partygoers work together to set up the tent they'll sleep in.

Scavenger Hunt Split the guests into two or three teams and give each team a list of ten to twenty items to find, such as a pine cone, an oak leaf, a 3" stick, a bug, a red pine needle, a marbled rock, and so on. Set a time limit and boundaries. The team with the most items on the list at the end of the hunt wins a prize for every team member.

Campfire The kids and parents work together to build a campfire. Then the kids cook hot dogs and s'mores over the campfire (a s'more is made by pressing two graham cracker squares together sandwich-style with a roasted marshmallow and a piece of a chocolate bar inside.)

Flashlight Tag This game is played like the traditional game of tag, except players become "it" when they're tagged by the beam of the flashlight.

Ha The guests lie on the ground in a circle, each laying her head on the stomach of the next child in the chain. The birthday child begins by saying, "ha." Then the next child in the circle says, "ha ha," and the next says, "ha ha ha." Keep going around the circle, adding a "ha" every time. See who will break the chain by laughing the wrong number of "ha's" on her turn.

Decorations

Decorate with strings of festive Christmas lights. If the party is held indoors, decorate the party room with a real tent or sheet-tents. Add stars and a moon dangling from the ceiling.

Cake

Make a sheet cake and create a tent for the top by leaning two graham crackers against each other and frosting them. Lay a small figurine inside the tent.

Party Favors

Miniature flashlights
Water bottles
Whistles
Trail mix

Cloud 9 Party

This heavenly party is a unique way for your daughter to celebrate her ninth birthday.
Age: 9

Invitations

Cut pale blue paper into the shape of a cloud and create a shimmery outline around the perimeter of the cloud using silver glitter glue. Glue small bits of cotton on the cloud, and write the party details in the center of the cloud beginning with, "Come Celebrate Abigail's Heavenly 9th Birthday on Cloud 9." Place cloud stickers on the outside of the envelope.

Activities

Cloud Book Before the party, get several large pieces of heavyweight, pale blue paper and draw a large cloud outline around the border of each page using silver glitter glue or a silver pen. Write a heading on each page, such as "Favorite Pizza Topping," "Favorite Movie," "Favorite Song," "Favorite

Teacher," "Favorite Ice Cream Flavor," "Favorite TV Show," "Favorite Book," "Favorite Music Group," "Favorite Color," "Hottest Movie Star," "Favorite Pastimes," and so on. As the guests arrive at the party, they join the others at a table and each guest signs the cloud sheets by recording their favorite item in each category and signing their first name. After the party, the birthday girl can organize the sheets into a booklet and keep the collection as a memento from her Cloud 9 party.

Cloud 9 Pillowcase Decorating Give each guest a plain white or pale blue pillowcase. Set out sponges, stamp pads, and stencils in the shapes of clouds, stars, and moons, along with fabric paint and fabric glitter. Let the kids autograph each other's pillowcases with a fabric pen and then paint the front of their own pillowcases using the fabric paint and shapes. Be sure to insert pieces of cardboard inside each pillowcase to prevent paint and pen from staining the other side as the pillowcases are decorated and autographed.

Heavenly Treasure Hunt Before the party, hide a small party favor for each guest in a designated area of the house or yard. Create a clue leading to each favor. The clues can be written in some type of code, such as Pig Latin, backwards writing (clues need to be held up to a mirror to be read), invisible ink (use a Q-tip or toothpick to write with lemon juice, which becomes visible once it's heated), or numerical codes (where each number corresponds with a letter of the alphabet). At the party, each guest draws a clue out of a hat, decodes the clue, and then finds the party favor.

Silver Lining Relay Race Divide the guests into two teams and give each team an empty pillowcase and a roll of tape. Line up the two teams and place two laundry baskets filled with books and magazines at the opposite end of the room or yard. Before the party, insert several large squares of tin foil throughout various pages of the books and magazines. At "Go!" the first guest on each team runs to the laundry basket, finds a piece of tin foil to place in her pillowcase, and runs back to the line. The guest hands the pillowcase to the next guest in line, who runs to the laundry basket and finds yet another silver square. Each team must continue collecting squares until they have nine squares, and then the teams must tape the nine squares together into one large square. The first team to have a completed nine-piece silver square (a silver lining) wins.

Ha The children lie on the floor in a circle, each laying her head on the stomach of the next child in the chain. The birthday child begins by saying, "ha." Then the next child in the circle says, "ha ha," and the next says, "ha ha ha." Keep going around the circle, adding a "ha" every time. See who will break the chain by laughing the wrong number of "ha's" on her turn.

Pass the Present Before the party, find a series of boxes that nest inside each other. In the smallest box, put a small gift for each guest, such as lip gloss. Wrap this box in cloud wrapping paper or light blue tissue paper, and then put this wrapped present in the next size box. Wrap this box, and keep going until the largest box is wrapped and you have a series of nested presents. At the party, have the kids sit on the floor in a circle and play music as the kids pass the present from one child to the next. When the music stops, the guest holding the box can unwrap it. If it's another wrapped box, start the music and have the kids pass the box again. Keep going until the final box is unwrapped, and then each guest gets a gift from the smallest box.

Decorations

Decorate the party room with light blue and white poster board cut into the shape of clouds, light blue and white balloons, tinsel, and white fluffy fiberfill stuffing scattered around the floor. Decorate the party table with fluffy cotton pieces, cloud-shaped place cards, silver Hershey kisses, and pale blue paper plates, napkins, cups, and hats. Decorate the birthday girl's party hat with silver glitter glue and a ring of white pom-poms or cotton around the rim and a single white pom-pom on top.

Cake

Serve light and airy angel food cake with strawberries, whipped cream, ice cream, sundae toppings, and iridescent candy sprinkles. Set up the toppings in a buffet and let each guest create her own angel food cake creation.

Party Favors

Decorated pillow cases
Light blue lip-gloss
Blue nail polish
Cloud pens
Pads of paper with cloud designs
3 Musketeers candy bars
Cloud stickers

Detective Party

Young detectives will have the opportunity to sharpen
their crime-solving skills at this party!
Ages: 9 to 12

Invitations

Fold heavyweight paper in half and cut it into miniature manila folders with tabs. The folders should be small enough to fit inside a small envelope. Write "Top Secret" on the outside cover of the folder and write the guest's name on the tab. Glue a piece of paper with the party details inside the folder. First write the invitation in backwards-writing that can be read only by holding the folder up to a mirror. Begin with, "Jared's Detective Agency needs your help to solve a crime," and then outline the party details. Create backwards writing by first writing the information in felt tip pen on a small piece of paper that will fit into the mini-folder. Then turn the paper over, and trace the writing onto the other side, making the writing backwards. Then glue the paper into the folder so that only the side with the backwards writing is showing. Mark the outside of the envelope with "?" "Confidential," or "Classified." The return address should read "Jared's Detective Agency."

Activities

Official Detective ID Card As guests arrive, they create a detective ID card. Give the guests each an index card or blank business card and ask them to select a code name such as Agent 99, Goldfinger, or 007 to write at the top of their card. Each guest then inks a finger on an inkpad and puts a fingerprint on the card. The guest must also complete other vital information on the card, such as eye color, favorite pizza topping, favorite color, favorite sport, favorite song, and so on. Laminate the ID cards with clear contact paper to make them look official.

Detective Memory Gather ten to fifteen household objects that could be linked to a crime, like a clock, a telephone, gloves, lipstick, tiny weapons from the game of Clue, a kitchen knife, a book of matches, a photograph, a mystery novel, and a bar of soap. Put the objects on a large tray and cover it with a cloth. Have the detectives sit in a circle on the floor, and give each of them a piece of paper and a pencil. Put the tray on the floor, and remove the cloth for about 30 seconds. Ask the kids to look carefully at everything on the tray. Then remove the tray, and ask them to write down from memory as many objects as they can remember. The child who remembers the highest number of objects wins a prize. Ask a bonus question, like what time did the clock read? Play a few rounds with different sets of household objects.

Missing Person A mysterious woman named Monique has hired Jared's Detective Agency to locate her long lost cousin, Jacques, who has inherited a large sum of money. Split the group into teams of about two or three detectives, and let the teams race against each other to be the first team to find Jacques. The teams will receive an identical set of clues, but each team will have its own color for the clues. For example, the red team's clues will be in red envelopes, the purple team's clues will be in purple envelopes, and the yellow team's clues will be in yellow envelopes. Each clue provides a piece of information about Jacques' whereabouts, and then leads the team to the next clue. Create a trail of clues that's age-appropriate for your guests. For example:

> CLUE #1: Give each team a balloon with a clue inside that says, "Jacques has said that he enjoys a view of the mountains to the east and a large island to the west from his waterfront home. Your next clue is under something soft." Hide the next clue under a sofa cushion.

> CLUE #2: Place a Canadian coin in an envelope. Write on the outside, "Jacques left this behind on his last visit to Monique. Your next clue is hidden in a cold place." Hide the next clue in the refrigerator.

> CLUE #3: "Monique's Caller ID shows that Jacques' phone number is 604-555-1190. Your next clue is someplace where you'll find more of these." Hide the next clue in the phone book.

> CLUE #4: Photocopy a map of Canada and the US that shows telephone area codes, including 604. "Jacques credit card bill shows that he buys tickets to see the Mariners and the Seahawks. Your next clue is attached to something reflective." Tape the next clue to a mirror.

> CLUE #5: "Jacques left a copy of his plane ticket behind on his last visit to Monique. It showed that he flew out of an airport with the abbreviation "POW." Your next clue is in an outdoor box." Hide the next clue in the mailbox.

CLUE #6: Photocopy a few detailed sections of a map of Canada and a map of your local area. Make sure that Jacques' town, Squirrel Cove, is shown on one of the maps, as well as the airport in Powell River. The other maps of Canada are included as decoys. "Jacques once said that his town is named after the small animals that are so abundant on his island. The distance between his town and Vancouver is equal to the distance between our town and Springfield (138 miles). Your next clue is under a meal location." Tape the next clue to the underside of the kitchen table.

CLUE #7: "Monique noticed a uniform in Jacques' suitcase on his last visit. She knows that he works for the government, but that his job is not dangerous. What town does Jacques live in, and where can he be found during the day? Write your answer below."

ANSWER: Jacques lives in Squirrel Cove, British Columbia, Canada. During the day, he can be found delivering the mail.

As the teams hand in their answers, award them with party favors. At parties for older children, make the clues more difficult by using codes, backwards writing, or pig latin. At parties for younger children, provide a more simple case to solve.

Murder Guests draw slips of paper out of a hat, and one is marked with a red X. That person is the murderer. The guests sit on the floor in a circle. The murderer tries to kill other guests by winking at them when he catches their eye. When another guest is the recipient of a wink, she falls dramatically on the floor as if she's been murdered and remains there until the end of the round. Meanwhile, the other guests watch each other to try to figure out who the murderer is. As soon as a guest catches the murderer winking at (murdering) another guest, he yells out the murderer's name. Play a few rounds.

Decorations

Draw body outlines on the driveway using sidewalk chalk. Cut out black construction paper footprints leading up to the door. Ask your local post office if they have any old "WANTED" posters of criminals that they can spare, and hang these in the party room. Place an empty jewelry box on the party table, along with a butter knife smeared with ketchup. Scatter play money on top of the party table.

Cake

Bake and frost a round layer cake. Arrange candies in the shape of a question mark on top of the cake.

Party Favors

Put the party favors in manila envelopes stamped "top secret," "private," "classified," "confidential," and "?"
Packs of gum
Miniature notepads labeled "Top Secret" and pencils
Inexpensive sunglasses
Fake noses
Children's mystery books
Official Detective ID Cards
Secret wrist storage pouches
Magnifying glasses

Starry Night Sleepover

*Provide the elements of fun for this creative sleepover party, and
the partygoers will take over and have a great time!*

Ages: 9 to 12

Invitations

Cut a star out of heavyweight paper and outline the edges with glitter glue.
Write, "Jessica's Starry Night Sleepover" on one side of the star and write the
party details on the other side.

Include a pickup time for the next morning and ask guests to bring a
sleeping bag.

Activities

Zipper Pulls As they arrive, the partygoers create beaded strands to tie to
their sleeping bag zipper pulls or hang from their backpacks. Lay out leather

cord and an assortment of beads. Tie a knot in the end of each cord and let the guests string the beads and tie the strands to their sleeping bag zippers.

Pillowcase Tie Dye Give each guest one white pillowcase, a clothespin, and elastics. Guests can create spiral designs by using clothespins to pinch the center of the pillowcase, winding it into a flat disk shape, and tightly wrapping elastics around it. They may also roll the pillowcase and tightly wrap a few elastics around the roll. Prepare a few different colors of fabric dye according to the directions on the box. The guests dip their pillowcases into buckets or bowls of the die, rinse, and repeat with another color on another section of the pillowcase. When the dyeing is complete, guests wash their pillowcases in a bucket of warm sudsy water, rinse them in cold water, and hang them up to dry.

Constellation Treasure Hunt Before the party, get one miniature flashlight for each guest. Tie on a label with the name of a constellation and hide the flashlights in various places in the yard or house. Create an age-appropriate clue to describe the hiding spot of each flashlight and write the clues in code. For example, you may use a white crayon that is legible only when watercolor paints are brushed over it, pig latin, backwards writing that can be read only by holding the clue up to a mirror, or lemon juice writing that becomes visible only after it's ironed. Write the name of a constellation on each clue too. For example, for a flashlight hidden in a cabinet under a sink, the clue might be: "Aquarius: Look Under a Source of Water." At the party, each guest draws a clue out of a bowl, deciphers the clue, and tries to find her hidden party favor.

Burglar Alarm The guests use the miniature pen flashlights from the Constellation Treasure Hunt in this game. Turn off the lights in the party room and have all the guests except one leave. The guest left behind sets the portable alarm clock to go off in five minutes, and hides it somewhere that's visible without moving anything in the room. The other guests return to the dark room with their miniature flashlights. They must hunt for the hidden alarm clock using their miniature flashlights, and try to find it before it goes off. The finder gets a turn to hide it next. If the clock goes off before it's found, then the hider hides it again.

Star Gazing Lay blankets on the lawn outside and have the kids lie down while they gaze at the stars and try to identify the Big Dipper, the Little Dipper, the North Star, and other constellations.

In the Bag One guest is "it" and leaves the room while the others each hide in a sleeping bag. "It" returns to the party room and picks a sleeping bag to feel. "It" tries to guess who is hidden in the sleeping bag. If "it" guesses correctly, than the hidden person becomes "it" next. If "it" guesses incorrectly, then "it" chooses another sleeping bag to guess.

Cookie Decorating Make cookie dough before the party or buy pre-made sugar cookie dough. At the party let the kids roll out a piece of dough and cut it into shapes of moons, stars and planets. Bake the cookies and then decorate with icing and sprinkles.

Bed Time Recording Before the party, prepare at least a dozen index cards with a thought-provoking question written on each one, such as, What's your favorite movie? What would you do if you won a million dollars? Where would you go if you had your own jet? What would you do if you were invisible? Who's your favorite movie star and why? What was your most embarrassing moment? While the guests are in another part of the house, slip a couple of index cards into each sleeping bag. When it's time to settle down, encourage the guests to look in their sleeping bags for the buried index cards. Once they're all in their sleeping bags, they can take turns reading their questions and talking about the answers. They can turn on a tape recorder and record their answers to play back over breakfast.

Waffle Sundae Bar The next morning, serve a fun breakfast of waffles and a variety of toppings and ice creams. Let the guests each create a waffle sundae for breakfast.

Decorations

Place glow-in-the-dark moons, stars, and planets around the sleeping room. Hang tinsel and cardboard stars wrapped in tinfoil from the doorway. Drape strings of holiday lights around the room. Put colored light bulbs in the lamps. Set up a mound of pillows in a corner of the room, complete with stuffed animals.

Cake

Weather permitting, set up a table outside. Wait until it's dark, and then take the cake outside and sing happy birthday in the dark to the glow of the birthday candles. Decorate the cake with icing outlines of the moon, stars, and planets, and sprinkle cake sparkles on top.

Party Favors

Tie-dye pillowcases
Pens with astronomy motif
Glow-in-the-dark stickers
Glow-in-the-dark super balls
Glow-in-the-dark plastic stars and planets
Astronomy books
Toothbrushes customized with names and star shapes using puff paints

Pool Party

If you have a pool, older children will have a blast at this active party!
Ages: 9 to 12

Invitations

Cut a rectangle of light blue colored paper using wavy scissors. Edge it with a black permanent marker. Draw a diving board at one end and add dark blue waves throughout the pool. Write "Dive Right in . . . to Sierra's Pool Party!" on the front and write the party details on the back. Ask guests to bring their bathing suits and towels.

Activities

Autograph Sheet Lay a flat, white bed sheet on the driveway and put out fabric pens and spray bottles filled with half water and half paint. As guests arrive, ask them to sign in by autographing the sheet and adding doodles and paint sprays. Hang the sheet on a clothesline. When it's dry, the autograph sheet can be used as a tablecloth at the party, and will be a nice memento for the birthday child after the party.

Water War Split the kids into teams and give each team a supply of sponges, water balloons, spray bottles, turkey basters, and cups. As a warm-up activity, partygoers soak the members of the opposite team.

Pool Dodge Ball Split the kids into two teams, the swimmers and the throwers. The swimmers go in the pool, and the throwers receive a supply of balls and sit on one edge of the pool. Be sure to use balls that are soft enough that they won't injure kids who are hit by them. The throwers throw the balls into the water at the swimmers as the swimmers try to dodge the thrown balls. When a swimmer is hit, he becomes a thrower and joins the other team on the edge of the pool and helps toss and retrieve balls. The last swimmer left in the pool wins. Continue playing several rounds.

Greasy Watermelon Grease a watermelon with a coating of Vaseline. Split the guests into two teams. Toss the watermelon into the center of the pool. The first team to bring the slippery watermelon to their side of the pool wins.

Sharks and Dolphins Rope off the shallow end and ask all guests to sit on the edge of the shallow end of pool, facing the rope. An adult stands at the rope. Split the guests into teams of three or four kids and give each team a name such as Sharks, Dolphins, Whales, Fish, Starfish, Crabs, Seaweed, and so on. The adult calls out team names one by one. As each team name is called out, the kids on that team must jump in the water and race across the shallow end to the other side of the rope without being tagged by the adult. Any kids who are tagged become helpers and try to tag other kids as they swim by.

Kids who reach the deep end successfully return to the edge of the shallow end and wait for their team name to be called again. When the adult yells, "Happy Birthday!" then all remaining players on the pool's edge must jump in and race to the finish line without getting tagged. The last remaining player wins. Continue playing several rounds.

Balloon Toss Each guest finds a partner. If there's an odd number of children, one guest can play the role of referee. The pairs stand in a straight line with partners facing each other, two feet apart. Each pair gets a filled water balloon. The referee (or adult) blows a whistle and the water balloons are tossed from one player to the other on each team. Any team that drops their water balloon is eliminated. The players all take one large step back away from each other. Then the referee blows the whistle again and the teams each toss their water balloons to the other players. Again, any team that drops their balloon is eliminated. Continue playing until there's only one winning team left.

Ice Cube Hunt Split the kids into two teams, such as the red team and the blue team, and toss a few dozen red and blue colored ice cubes into the pool. The teams race to collect twenty of their ice cubes before they melt.

Keep It Dry Split the guests into two teams and give each team a bowl of cotton balls, one for each team member. Place these bowls on the edge of the pool's shallow end, and put two empty bowls at the opposite end of the pool. One at a time, the kids swim the length of the pool while holding a cotton ball in the air, trying to keep the cotton ball dry. Dry cotton balls are deposited in the empty bowl at the other end of the pool. Once all guests have taken their turns, the number of dry cotton balls in each team's second bowl is counted, and the team with the highest number wins.

Water Basketball Divide the kids into two teams and play water basketball until one team scores five baskets.

Kickboard Relay Race Split the kids into two teams and give each team a kickboard. Kids race from one end of the pool to the next, then give the kickboard to the next guest in line. The first team to finish wins.

Balloon Polo Set up a water polo net. Divide the kids into two teams and give them a water balloon. The teams toss the water balloon back and forth over the net, trying to catch it before it hits the water and pops. Teams earn points when the opposing team lets the balloon pop. Continue playing until one team has ten points.

Sixty-eight Cents Split the guests into teams of three or four players. Throw several coins into the shallow end of the pool. The teams try to collect the right coins to total precisely sixty-eight cents. Each team may have no more than seven coins in their pile at any one time. The first team with sixty-eight cents wins.

Decorations

Select balloons and paper goods in different shades of blue for this party. Decorate the party table with a grouping of suspended beach balls, or dangle beach balls from the trees and from the pool fence.

Cake

Decorate a sheet cake to look like a swimming pool with a wafer cookie diving board, blue frosting, mini beach chairs and umbrellas, and people figurines. If the party's held during lunchtime or dinnertime, set up a grill and have a cookout.

Party Favors

Miniature bottles of sunscreen and sun protection for lips
Whistles
Goggles
Sunglasses
Water bottles
Beach balls

Parties for All Ages

Art Party

Kids of all ages will enjoy this party's activities!
Ages: 2 to 9

Invitations

Cut heavy white paper into the shape of a palette, and glue circles of color onto it. Write, "Taylor's Art Party!" on the palette front, and note the party details on the back. Use dabs of watercolor paint to decorate the back of the outer envelope. You could add an outline of the birthday child's hand to the back of the envelope as well.

Activities

Paint the House (age 2) Give each 2-year-old a bucket filled with water and a foam paintbrush. Let the guests paint the outside of your house with water.

Art Party

Contact Art (ages 2 and 3) Cut clear contact paper into 8 ½" x 11" pieces (approximately) and tape these to a table with the sticky side facing up. Cut small shapes out of colored paper and put these as well as big chunks of sparkly confetti on paper plates around the table. As guests arrive, they sprinkle and attach the colorful pieces to the clear contact paper. When they're done, an adult attaches a large piece of colored paper to the top, sealing the artwork.

Plaster Painting Purchase a variety of plaster objects, paint, and paintbrushes. Squirt several colors of paint onto a few paper plates. The guests each select a plaster piece to paint, and when they're done, an adult adds a coat of clear glossy spray paint.

Fabric Mural Hang a plain sheet from a clothesline and give guests squirt bottles and spray bottles filled with fabric paint. The children squirt paint all over the sheet. Toward the end of the party, lay the sheet down on the ground and provide fabric pens for guests to autograph the sheet and add doodles. The sheet will be a great memento for the birthday child and can be used as a tablecloth at future birthday parties.

Letter Decorating At a craft store, buy wooden alphabet letters that are a few inches tall. Select one letter for each guest, the first letter of his name. At the party, set the letters out on a table along with glitter glue, wiggle eyes, pipe cleaners, markers, and mini-stickers, and let the guests decorate their letters.

T-shirt Decorating Kids decorate plain white T-shirts with handprints, sponge prints (cut sponges in various shapes or buy pre-cut art sponges), or stencil shapes using fabric paint and fabric pens. You can help the kids paint their names on their T-shirts. You can substitute a pair of socks, a pillowcase, or a bandana/scarf for this activity.

Mini Painting Children paint a miniature watercolor painting on a 4"x 6" piece of paper. When it dries, slip it into a plastic picture frame with a magnet on the back and give it as a party favor.

Body Collage Get a large roll of paper and cut it into body-size sheets. Have each guest lay down on a sheet of paper while an adult traces the outline of his body. Give the kids washable markers, paints, crayons, magazines, scissors, and glue sticks to decorate their images. As an alternative, kids can create self-portraits on the driveway using sidewalk chalk.

Placemat Art Give each guest a piece of colorful poster board or construction paper with his name stenciled on the bottom. Give the kids glue sticks, washable markers, crayons, stickers, and photos cut out from magazines, and ask them to decorate their place mats. Once they're done, cover the place mats with clear contact paper or laminating paper. Use them as place mats at the party and then let the kids take them home as party favors.

Artist Relay Race (ages 6 and up) Split the kids into two teams and establish a starting line and a goal, which should be a wall. Tape or tack two big sheets of paper at the goal, and give a marker to the first child in each line. The first child in each line must run to his or her team's sheet of paper, draw a happy face, run back to the line with the marker, and hand the marker off to the next child in line. That child then runs to the piece of paper and draws another happy face, and so on. The first team to have drawn a full family of happy faces on the sheet of paper wins.

Watercolor Hunt (ages 6 to 8) Before the party, hide party favors for each guest in different locations. Then write the location of each hiding place on a different piece of paper using a white crayon. (For pre-readers, you can draw a picture of the hiding location.) The paper will look blank because the white crayon doesn't show. At the party, the kids each take a piece of paper and paint it with watercolors until the white crayon writing is visible. Then they go find their hidden party favors.

Cookie Painting Before the party, bake sugar cookies in various shapes using cookie cutters (pre-made refrigerated dough sold at the grocery store works fine). Create cookie paints by mixing two egg whites with a teaspoon of water and dividing the mixture into several cupcake tins (some grocery stores sell pasteurized egg whites). Add a different food coloring to each one. The kids use clean paintbrushes to paint the cookies in various colors and patterns. Give each partygoer an award for his or her cookies, such as "Most Colorful," "Most Delicious-Looking," "Most Beautiful," "Most Festive," "Most Artistic," and so on.

Bottle Cap Pins Before the party, spray paint twist-off bottle caps with a base coat of acrylic paint. Use a glue gun to attach a pin to the back. Provide paints and paintbrushes and let guests create designs such as ladybugs, stars, flowers, hearts, suns, and swirls on the bottle caps.

Friendship Bracelets Provide cording and beads and let the guests weave friendship bracelets.

Paper Match Wrap each party favor in different wrapping paper, attach a helium balloon, and scatter the presents around the yard or party room. Cut a small square of each wrapping paper. Put the squares of wrapping paper into a bowl and let the kids draw a piece of wrapping paper from the bowl. They match this up with the paper wrapping on one of the party favors, and that's their favor.

Decorations

Hang large paintbrushes from the party room ceiling. Cover the party table with plain white paper and put a few cups of crayons or markers on the table so guests can decorate the tablecloth.

Cake

Bake a round cake and cut it into the shape of a palette. Frost the background white, add round circles of colors with gel icing, stick a paintbrush into the cake, and use crayon candles. Serve the cake with room temperature 7-Up or Sprite, and give the kids an assortment of colored ice cubes to drop into their water. Make the colored ice cubes before the party by adding food coloring to water. The kids will enjoy watching the colors mix as their ice cubes melt into their drinks.

Party Favors

Personalized T-shirts
Paintbrushes
Paints
Painted cookies
Magnetic plastic frames and mini paintings
Placemats
Markers
Coloring books
Pads of drawing paper

Nature Party

Explore and enjoy the great outdoors in this back-to-nature celebration.
Ages: 3 to 10

Invitations

Make a simple and natural invitation by cutting envelope-sized rectangles out of a brown paper grocery bag using zigzag scissors, punching holes around the outside edges, and threading paper or raffia ribbon through the holes. Write the party details in the center with a black permanent marker.

Activities

Nature Bags Give each guest a paper bag with his name stenciled on it. Provide markers, stickers, objects from nature such as leaves and pine needles, and tempera paints in paper plates. The kids decorate their bags with markers, stickers, and stamp designs created by dipping the nature objects into the paint and pressing the shapes on the bag. As an alternative, the children may use sponges or stamps in the shapes of leaves, vines, flowers, or trees. The nature bags can be used to take home party favors.

Bird Feeders The guests make their own peanut-butter-pinecone bird feeders. Before the party, gather one pinecone for each guest and attach a piece of wire or string to its top so it can be hung from a tree. At the party, lay out plastic knives and paper plates with peanut butter and birdseed. Let the guests smear peanut butter on their pinecones and sprinkle them with birdseed. Put the finished bird feeders in plastic bags for the guests to take home and hang in their yards.

Planting Before the party, dig one hole in your yard for each child. At the party, give each child a cup of fertilizer, a cup of water, and a small plant and show them how to place their plants in the ground.

Nature Walk Take the kids on a walk in nearby woods or a hiking trail. Give each child a bag to collect objects—such as pine needles, pinecones, pebbles, sticks, acorns, wildflowers, and leaves—for their nature collages.

Spot the Wildlife Ask guests to point out any wildlife they see while they're on the Nature Walk. Give out a small party favor (or stamp hands with a small stamp and washable ink) every time a guest spots a different animal.

Rock Creatures While on the Nature Walk, ask each child to find a fist-sized rock to take back to the house to decorate. Wash the rocks as a group. Set out paints, permanent markers, glitter glue, wiggly eyes, yarn, mini pom-poms, pipe cleaners, glue, or other supplies, and let the kids decorate their rocks to look like creatures. Make a sample rock creature before the party and have a few extra rocks on hand.

Nature Party

Nature Collage When the kids return from the Nature Walk, give each child a piece of construction paper and put out glue and markers. Help the kids trace their hands onto the paper. Then they fill in their hand shape, by gluing the nature objects they collected onto the page (you might want to have some extra objects on hand in case kids run out).

Name That Plant Before the party, attach pictures of various flowers, trees, bushes, and plants to index cards. At the party, have the kids sit on the floor in a circle. Hold the index cards up one by one and have the kids guess the name of each plant. Kids can yell out their guesses, and correct guesses are rewarded with a sticker.

Nature Concentration (ages 8 and up) Place about ten objects from nature on a tray and cover it with a towel. Give each guest a piece of paper and a pencil. Remove the towel, show them the tray, and let them study the objects on the tray for a couple minutes. Then take the tray away and ask the guests to write down as many objects as they can remember. Review the lists as a group and give a prize to the guest with the most objects on his list. Play another round with a different set of objects.

Nature Scavenger Hunt (ages 7 and up) Split the guests into teams of three or four guests, and give each team the same list of objects from nature to find. Set a time limit and boundaries, and reward a prize to the team that has collected the most items on the list when time's up. A simpler version of this hunt can be created for pre-readers by using pictures instead of words for the items on the list, and keeping the game very simple.

Piñata Fill a brown paper grocery bag with candy, snacks, and small toys. Tape the top closed and run a string through it to hang it from the ceiling. Decorate it with objects from nature, such as pinecones, pine needles, grass, sticks, and flowers, as well as ribbons and streamers. Have the kids take turns hitting it with a bat until the bag breaks and the treats fall to the ground.

Decorations

Decorate the walkway to your door with a trail of birdseed. Decorate the party room with plants, flowers, baskets of pinecones, and large branches from outdoor trees. Perch toy birds on the branches.

Cake

Serve "dirt" in small clay or plastic pots. Wash the pots and line them with foil. Fill them with softened ice cream and sprinkle crushed Oreo's on top. Freeze them until it's time to sing "Happy Birthday," then toss in a gummy worm and add a flower on a stick. Place birthday candles in the birthday child's dirt.

Party Favors

Plants
Decorated rocks
Birdseed
Nature stickers
Bird feeders
Seed packets

Pizza Party

Before making the pizza, guests must hunt for the pizza ingredients in a unique treasure hunt! It's a great celebration for junior chefs of all ages.

Ages: 3 to 10

Invitations

Cut a large piece of construction paper into a large circle and let the birthday child decorate it with pizza toppings using glue sticks and markers, paints, or small shapes of colored paper. Cut the pizza into slices and print the party details on the back of each pizza slice. Write, "Jade's Pizza Party!" on the front. If you're hand-delivering the invitations, ask your local pizza place for some small empty pizza boxes and place each invitation inside a box. Glue a paper with the words "Hot! Hot! Hot! You're invited to Jade's Pizza Party!" to the outside of each box.

Activities

Apron Decorating Buy plain aprons or dish towels and set them out on a table with fabric paints, sponge shapes, and fabric markers. The kids decorate their aprons or dish towels with handprints, doodles, shapes, and autographs. An alternative for younger kids is to cut small apron shapes from poster board and let the kids decorate them with stickers, markers, confetti, and glue sticks.

Pizza-Topping Treasure Hunt Before the party, hide several items that are used for pizza toppings such as a tomato, a stick of pepperoni, a pepper, an onion, a bunch of garlic, and a can of tomato sauce. Create clues for the children to find the toppings. If the kids are too young to read, draw a picture or take a Polaroid photo of the hiding spot for each topping. At the party, have the kids each draw a clue out of a hat, then go find their topping and bring it back to the kitchen. Once the ingredients have all been found, the group can move on to the next activity. For older kids, make the pizza-topping hunt a scavenger hunt and break the kids into teams. Send them to a designated area of your house or yard to find as many hidden toppings as they can within fifteen minutes.

Make Individual Pizzas Buy or make fresh pizza dough, and give each guest a little ball of dough to knead and roll with a pin. (To make it simpler for younger kids, you can give them the pre-cooked pizza dough or bagels and limit the activity to topping them.) Set up bowls of toppings, such as cheese, tomato sauce, pepperoni, onions, hamburger, peppers, olives, sausage, and so on, and have kids assemble their own pizzas. While the pizza is cooking, serve room temperature 7-Up or Sprite in clear glasses along with colorful ice cubes made from water that's been tinted with food coloring. The kids will have fun watching the ice cubes melt in their drinks.

Pass the Present Before the party, find a series of boxes that nest inside each other. In the smallest box, place a small present for each guest. Wrap this box, then put it inside the next size box. Wrap this box, and keep going until the largest box is wrapped. At the party, while the pizzas are cooking, have the kids sit on the floor in a circle. Play music as the kids pass the present from one child to the next. When the music stops, the kid holding the box can unwrap it. If it's another wrapped box, start the music, and the box gets passed again. Keep going until the final box is unwrapped, and then each child gets a party favor from the smallest box.

Pizza, Pizza, Pepperoni Play like Duck, Duck, Goose, but substitute types of pizza.

Pizza Piñata Make a Piñata out of a pizza box. Fill the box with candy and small toys and seal it closed with tape. Decorate it with red and white streamers and balloons and suspend it with string. Let the kids take turns poking it with a broomstick until the tape gives way and the goodies fall out.

Decorations

Decorate the party room like a pizza parlor. Use red-and-white checkered tablecloths and play guitar music. Decorate with red-and-white balloons and use solid red plates, cups, and napkins.

Cake

Bake a giant round chocolate chip cookie by pressing cookie dough into a round pie plate or pizza pan. Decorate to look like a pizza using frosting strands (or coconut) and colorful candies. Serve with ice cream, hot fudge, whipped cream, and toppings. Let the kids make cookie sundaes.

Party Favors

Pizza stickers

Mini rolling pins

Decorated aprons or dish towels

Pizza crust recipes

Wrap the party favors in a piece of red-and-white checked fabric. Twist at the top and tie a ribbon around it.

Olympics Celebration

This party is an outdoor celebration for the active birthday child, although several games will work indoors if the weather becomes inclement. In good weather, the party can be held at a nearby field or in your yard.

Ages: 5 to 12

Invitations

Start with a rectangle of heavyweight white paper. Fold it and draw the Olympic rings symbol on the outside cover by tracing outlines of quarters with markers. Write, "Calling All Champs! You're Invited to Celebrate Tyler's Birthday at His Olympics Celebration!"

Activities

Bodybuilder Contest While you're waiting for all the guests to arrive, ask the children to warm up their lungs by blowing up a few dozen balloons.

Once everyone has arrived, split the group into teams of two or three and give each team a set of oversized clothing for one team member to wear. At "Go!" the teams race to dress one team member in the oversized clothing and then to stuff as many balloons as possible inside the clothing, making the guest look like a body builder. When time's up, count the number of balloons inside each body builder's outfit. The team that stuffed the highest number of balloons wins a gold medal (use gold chocolate coins) for each team member.

Crossfire This non-competitive warm-up game is ideal to play across a driveway. Split the children into two teams. One team stands on one side of the driveway, and the other team stands on the other side. The birthday child is "it" in the first round and stands in the center of the driveway. When "it" calls "Run!" the children on both sides of the driveway run to the other side of the driveway while "it" tries to tag them. Anyone who gets tagged joins "it" in the center of the driveway for the next round and helps "it" tag the other children. Keep playing until there's only one runner left. That player becomes "it" in the next round.

Team Obstacle Course Split the group into two teams and provide each team with a set of household objects, such as boxes, cones, trash cans, baskets, hoses, bottles, pillows, chairs, rope, a bell to ring, etc. With the supervision of an adult, each team builds an obstacle course in a separate area of the yard. Once the two obstacle courses are complete, each team demonstrates their obstacle course for the other team. Then each team runs through the other team's course. Time the kids running through the obstacle courses and post the times on a poster board. The team with the fastest average time wins. Give each member on that team a gold chocolate coin. If there will be more than twelve children at the party, consider splitting them into three teams.

Olympics Celebration

Tug of War Set up a tug of war over a kiddie pool. Play three rounds, and award gold chocolate medals to the winning team.

Egg Toss Split the kids into pairs. Give each pair a raw egg, and have them stand a few feet apart from each other (older kids may start further apart from each other, such as on either side of a driveway), and toss the egg back and forth. The pair with the most successful tosses without breaking the egg wins a gold chocolate medal.

Discus Throw Line the guests up and ask them to throw a Frisbee as far as they can. Give the three children with the longest throws a gold chocolate medal.

Dodge Ball Split the kids into two teams. One team stands in a circle and the other team stands inside. The team that formed the circle takes turns throwing the ball (use a large, soft ball) at the children inside the circle. When a child gets hit by the ball, then he joins the team forming the circle. The last child left inside the circle wins a gold chocolate medal. Play again, and let the teams switch starting positions. (For a non-competitive version of this game, have the successful thrower replace the person he hit. For large groups, you can use two or three balls simultaneously.)

Bull's Eye Toss Spread out target baskets (or buckets or bowls) and assign a point value to each basket. Let the guests stand behind the starting line, and give each child five Tootsie Rolls to throw into the baskets. Count the number of points they earn. Keep score on a poster board. The children can keep any candy that lands in a basket, and the three children with the highest number of points win gold chocolate medals.

Chariot Relay Race Divide the kids into two teams, and give each team a chariot (a wagon or a wheelbarrow). Establish a starting line and a goal. Each guest must push another guest in the chariot around the goal and back to the starting line, then hand the chariot over to the next pair in line. The first team to finish wins. Award gold chocolate medals to everyone on the winning team.

Three-Legged Race Pair up the guests and give each a length of rope. Standing side-by-side, each pair ties the two inside legs together at the ankle. Establish a starting line and a finish line, and let the pairs race each other to the finish line. The winning pair receives gold chocolate coins.

Sack Race Guests step into old pillowcases and race each other by hopping from the starting line to the finish line.

Awards Ceremony After each event, award the winning team, pair, or individual a chocolate gold coin. At the end of the entire Olympic meet, count the number of gold medals that each guest has accumulated. Award overall gold, silver, and bronze medals or party favors for the first, second, and third place winners of the day. Award all of the other guests a copper medal for good sportsmanship.

Decorations

Decorate with an all-American color scheme with American flags, red, white, and blue streamers and balloons, and party goods from Independence Day.

Cake

Olympic Cake Draw the Olympic symbol on a sheet cake using different colors of icing.

Party Favors

Chocolate gold coins given out after each event
Medals
Super balls
Jump ropes
Whistles
Decorative shoelaces
Sweatbands
Water bottles
Team T-shirts or tank tops
Soft footballs
Whiffleball sets
Sports caps

Grand Slam Baseball Bash

There are so many ways to celebrate at a baseball party—other than playing baseball! Some of these activities can be played indoors in case of inclement weather.

Ages: 5 to 12

Invitations

Cut heavy, white paper in a circle and decorate it with red stitching using a marker. On the baseball, write, "Come to Daniel's Grand Slam Baseball Bash!" Write the party details on the back.

Activities

Baseball Card Making If you have a home computer that includes a scanner, you can create a baseball card for each of your child's friends before the party, personalized with their photos. Leave the vital stats on the back blank (eye color, favorite pizza, favorite player, favorite team, etc.) and let the guests fill these out and pick a team sticker to attach to the front.

Hat Decorating Buy inexpensive painter's caps and let the kids decorate them with fabric pens and fabric paints as they arrive. Older children may enjoy autographing each other's caps.

Home Run Derby Designate a section of the yard or field as the home run territory. Pitch a Whiffleball to each partygoer five times to see how many home runs he hits. The other guests field the hits. Give a special prize to the guest who hits the most home runs. Also have each fielder count the number of balls they catch on the fly, and award a prize to the fielder with the most outs.

Whiffleball If there are at least eight guests, play a three-inning Whiffleball game. Split the kids into teams by having them draw jelly beans from a bowl. The kids who draw red jelly beans are on the Red Sox team and the kids who draw white jelly beans are on the White Sox team.

Whiffleball Toss (indoors or outdoors). Place three boxes (designated first base, second base, and third base) several feet from a pitching line. Give each kid a chance to toss four Whiffleballs into the boxes. They earn one point for a single, two points for a double, and three points for a triple. And if they get a ball in each box, they get a two-point bonus. The guest with the most points wins a special prize, such as a pack of baseball cards.

Baseball Relay Race Split the group into two teams and set up a starting line and a goal line with two chairs. Give each team a baseball and a spoon. At "Go!" the first player in each team places the baseball in the spoon and runs with it down to the chair, circles the chair, and returns to line to hand off the spoon and the baseball to the next player. If the ball is dropped, the player must start over. The first team to have every player take a turn wins.

By the Numbers The kids stand in a circle, with one child in the center holding the baseball. Each guest is given a number, and the child in the center throws the baseball high into the air, calling out a number as he does so. The guest with that number must catch the fly ball before it hits the ground. If he's successful, then he throws the ball into the air, calling another number. If the called fielder is unsuccessful, then the child throwing the ball into the air does it again. Younger children may be more successful at this game if a larger ball is used, about the size of a soccer ball, and if an adult calls out the numbers.

Dodge Baseball Split the kids into two teams. One team makes a circle and the other team stands inside. The team that formed the circle takes turns throwing the ball (use a soft, spongy softball) at the kids inside the circle. When a guest gets hit by the ball, he joins the team forming the circle. The last kid left inside the circle wins a gold medal. Play again, and let the teams switch starting positions.

Baseball Card Hunt Hide several dozen baseball cards around a room in the house or in the yard. Let the kids pick up as many cards as they can find. At the end, the guest with the most cards wins a special prize. All the kids can keep their cards.

Flipping Cards Using the cards that the guests gathered in the last activity, let them each lean five or so cards up against a wall, hold the rest, and stand behind a line that's a few feet away. At "Go!" each guest flicks the cards they're holding at the cards leaning against the wall, attempting to topple them over. The first guest to knock over all five cards wins.

Ice Cream Truck Arrange for an ice cream truck to visit, or create one using your car. Give the partygoers play money to pay for their ice creams.

Decorations

Use red, white, and blue balloons, streamers, and tableware to decorate the party room. Scatter baskets of peanuts around the room.

Cake

Frost a round cake with white icing, then decorate it with red icing seams to look like a giant baseball. For snacks, serve mini hot dogs in a blanket, or ballpark franks.

Party Favors

Place the party favors in small brown paper bags labeled "peanuts" and sealed with a baseball sticker.
Baseball cards
Baseball gumdrops
Pencils with baseballs or baseball erasers
Baseball stickers
Peanuts in shells
Super balls
Baseball caps
Bubble gum
Water bottles

Holding Fun Parties Outside the Home

Holding Fun Parties Outside the Home

The possibilities for parties held outside the home are endless. The key is to find a location that is interesting to your child and yet special or unusual in some way, and then to build a theme around a party in that location. A few ideas are listed below to get you started.

Some of the facilities will have someone on staff to lead the activities at your child's birthday party. If that's the case, it's always a good idea to meet with that person before finalizing your party plans. Make sure that person is experienced at running successful children's birthday parties and, if you can, observe another party before booking your child's. Ask about the best times for the party so that the atmosphere won't be too chaotic at the time of your child's party.

Whether the facility will run the party or you will, make it special by adding your own personal touches. For example, at a gymnastics studio party, hand out personalized medals at the end of the party to recognize each child's best event. For a miniature golf party, bring index cards with "stunt putts" written on them (such as putting the ball through the legs of the other children) and have one guest draw a card at each hole. Bring a video camera to a bowling party and conduct on-air interviews after the match. Hand out awards at a ceramics studio for the most colorful piece, the most artistic piece, the most creative painter, the fastest painter, the most talkative painter, the happiest painter, and so on. Play Red Rover or Duck, Duck, Goose on skates at an ice rink or roller skating rink. At a zoo party, give each child a pencil and an index card with the letters of "Happy Birthday, Sean" spelled vertically down the left side, and challenge the guests to come up with as many animal names as they can beginning with each of the letters in that phrase. (For example, next to "H" they can write hippopotamus, next to "A" they can write aardvark, next to "P" they can write python, and so on, based on the animals at the zoo.) Peruse the ideas throughout this book to see which can be adapted to a party held outside the home.

Party favors may reflect the theme at parties held outside the home, too. For example, hand out ballet coloring books at the ballet studio party. At the gymnastics studio, hand out water bottles and wrist sweatbands. At a museum party, hand out passes to the museum or post cards from the museum gift shop. At a movie theatre party, use empty popcorn boxes to hold each guest's party favors. At the zoo party, wrap the party favors in a piece of leopard-spotted or zebra-striped fabric.

Invitations can reflect the location of the party in a unique way. For example, invitations can be a piece of colored paper cut into the shape of a building, with a sign drawn on the building stating the name of the facility. Invitations could also look like a large ticket with "Admit One" written on the front, and the party details written on the back. Some party locations will provide invitations as part of their birthday package. Make sure you specify on the invitation that parents should drop off and pick up kids at the facility.

Check to make sure that the facility will have a private room or area for the kids to sing Happy Birthday and to enjoy cake. If it's allowed, you may want to add some decorative touches of your own to this room, like streamers, a birthday throne, and a photograph of the birthday child at birth.

Here are some options for locations of parties held outside the home:

- Gymnastics studio
- Plaster art, ceramic studio, or pottery studio
- Museum (Children's Museum, Science Museum, Computer Museum, Art Museum)
- Theater or movies
- Miniature golf
- Health club
- Roller skating rink or ice skating rink
- Zoo
- Animal farm
- Aquarium
- Amusement park or water park
- Dance studio
- Hotel pool

Holding Fun Parties Outside the Home

- Karate studio
- Ice cream parlor
- Bowling alley
- Arcade
- Pet shop
- Go-kart track
- Hair salon
- Pizza parlor
- Day care or pre-school facility
- Playground
- Park
- Hiking trail
- Billiards
- Batting cages
- Hotel suite

I'd Like to Hear from You!
....

Please drop me a line to let me know how you used this book and to share your new party ideas. Which ideas in this book worked best for you? Which party themes did you use? What new party themes would you like to see? How did you adapt the parties in this book? I'd love to hear all about your child's birthday party! Please send an e-mail to sbaltrus@attbi.com. Many thanks!

—Susan Baltrus

About the Author

   Susan Baltrus is the author of *Thinking Games for Preschoolers,* as well as several articles in trade magazines and journals. A teacher, researcher, author, and mother of three, Susan loves to share her creative ideas with other parents and has recently been in demand as a birthday party consultant. She holds a B. S. degree in communications, marketing, and quantitative methods, and lives with her family in Massachusetts.

Additional copies of this book and other titles published by
RiverOak publishing are available from your local bookstore.

If you have enjoyed this book, or if it has impacted your life,
we would like to hear from you.

Please contact us at:

RiverOak Publishing
Department E
P.O. Box 700143
Tulsa, Oklahoma 74170-0143
Or by e-mail at info@riveroakpublishing.com

Visit our website at:
www.riveroakpublishing.com